Climbing Plants

SMALL GARDEN LIBRARY

Climbing Plants

Richard Gorer

Studio Vista

ACKNOWLEDGMENTS

Grateful acknowledgment is given to the following for permission to use their photographs: to Dr T. S. Stone for all the colour transparencies; to Mr A. J. Huxley for 4, 5, 6, 11, 19, 20, 21, 27; to Mr Dennis Woodland for 3, 12, 13, 14, 29, 30; to Mr J. E. Downward for 22; to Bernard Alfieri Ltd for 28.

Published in 1968 by Studio Vista Limited
Blue Star House, Highgate Hill, London N19

Set and printed in 10 pt Imprint

Made and printed in Great Britain by
The Garden City Press Limited
Letchworth, Hertfordshire

SBN 289 37083 3

Contents

Preface

If building ground is at a premium, you build skyscrapers. If you have only so much room you must get the best possible out of it. Similarly if your garden is too small to grow all the plants you want on the flat, you must start thinking about growing upwards. To the right and to the left are the boundary fences, but vertically the sky's the limit. No one has yet decided how small a small garden is, but if you are a plantsman, you can be fairly sure that it is too small. We should distinguish I think between gardeners and plantsmen. You can make a garden without any flowers at all and there are some famous Japanese gardens that do just that. A lot of sand raked into attractive patterns and few well chosen rocks can make a Japanese garden that has become world famous. If, however, you wish to grow plants, space becomes more important. Once you have filled all that is available, you can only go upwards.

This is where the climbing plants come to your assistance. They will provide plant cover for a lot of sites that might otherwise be eyesores. We need fuel stores and potting sheds; we may even have oil tanks and though all these erections are necessary, they are not ornamental. Climbers will not only disguise these eyesores, they may even turn them into things of beauty. Our boundaries will be composed of fences or hedges; we can make these more interesting by the judicious use of climbing plants. Moreover there is no need to be niggardly Once one climber is established it will support a second one. If you want to grow plenty of plants and are restricted on the ground, climbers will help to solve your problems.

In the following chapters you will find mentioned (I hope) every climbing plant that can be grown in this country. Only a large Botanic Garden would attempt to grow them all, but from this list you may find the plant that will suit you. Some are too vigorous for very small gardens, others may be too tender for your locality, but somewhere you should find what you need.

1 May I introduce

The one character that all climbers have in common is that they depend on other plants for support in order to reach the light. The methods that they use differ, but they can be summarized fairly accurately under four headings. The first, and I suppose the least efficient, are those plants that do little except lean on their hosts. These are represented in gardens by the various climbing roses. They start off by throwing up a fairly thick and rigid stem, but this elongates to such an extent that, if it has not got into a tree or other support, it will eventually fall flat on the ground. The prickles help to support the branches, once they have got up into the supporting tree, but they are only a contribution and they will not support the branch if it has not grown into a suitable position. There are not many of these climbers.

The second type is represented by those plants that develop special roots or other appendages which adhere to the surface and support their stems in this way. The best known of these plants is the ivy, but there are others, such as a few hydrangeas and such plants as schizophragma and pileostegia. Bridging the gap between this section and the next is the popular Virginian Creeper, parthenocissus. This has tendrils, but a number of adhesive disks are formed at the end of these tendrils, so that the plant can support itself on a surface that would be too large to be circled by a tendril.

This leads us easily to the third type of climber which supports itself by means of clutching on to its support either by means of specially developed modifications of the leaves, known as tendrils, or by twisting the leaf stems. The popular Sweet Pea exemplifies the first type and the equally popular Clematis or tropaeolum serve to illustrate the second.

Finally there are the plants that twine round their hosts. This seems the most popular way of climbing, among temperate plants at any rate, and examples can range from the infuriating bindweed to the exquisite *Schizandra rubrifolia*.

One might think that a knowledge of how a climber climbs would be essential in deciding where to place any particular plant in the garden. I would certainly think so myself, but generally this information is not given by nurserymen in their catalogues and it is not always easy to obtain in other horticultural publications. Whatever the other imperfections of this volume, this particular lack will be filled. When we come to discuss the various climbers, they will be listed according to their method of climbing.

The fact that a plant is a climber will tell us something about its requirements in the garden. If a plant has to climb it means that its roots will be in the shade, and if its roots are in the shade it indicates that the temperature there will be comparatively cool. Will it also be moist? Not necessarily. Some trees, birch is a notorious example, absorb so much water that the soil beneath them is often parched to a surprising degree. Against this must be placed the facts that the shade does prevent rapid evaporation and that the continued rotting of the fallen leaves should have a mulching effect. Of course in the garden, the dead leaves are tidied away and we should make allowance for that, when looking after our climbers. At any rate we can assume that what a climber requires is a shady and cool root run and, preferably, one that will not dry out too much.

Most large climbers are dependent on forest trees for their support in the wild and are therefore used to a soil rich in humus, but the smaller plants, which would scramble through scrub or maquis, may well be used to rather poor rocky soil. It is in this sort of soil that most clematis species grow and for these and similar plants rich soil is not necessarily advantageous, although it never does any harm.

The type of climbing that the plant employs will also indicate the most desirable position. The enormous roses of the *Synstylae*, *Rosa filipes*, *R. helenae*, *R. longicuspis*, etc., are really only suitable for growing among large trees. When established these are extremely vigorous plants, quite capable of making twenty feet of growth in a season, and they would be far too vigorous for growing on a wall, quite apart from the tedium and difficulty of tying in the branches. On the other hand, self-clingers like *Hydrangea petiolaris* are very suitable for walls and if required for growing up trees must be trained to the trunk, up which they will creep. Climbers with tendrils must have a lot of rather fine twigs or wire to support them. If you want to get a Clematis into a tree, you will have to support it for the first part of its life. This is usually done by tying it to a cane. Once the plant is tall enough to reach the twiggy portions of the tree or shrub, it can be left to support itself. It is not very often that the large-flowered Clematis are used in this manner, but vigorous plants like *C. montana* will often do better and be more spectacular when allowed to ramp in this way.

The same thing applies to the twining climbers. Here again it is best to let them ascend a cane until they reach a height where the support is not too large to be twined round. The trunk of a tree, if it is of any size, is too large. The plant gets discouraged and fails to ascend; instead it will start growing along the ground in search of something more suitable.

The most obvious situation in the garden for climbers is the walls of the house, but it will now be appreciated that, except for ivies and similar self-clingers, some sort of framework must be provided on which the climbers can support themselves. With those plants that support themselves with tendrils, or their equivalent, some sort of netting is the most suitable. The tendency nowadays is to use a mesh of green or black-coloured plastic. This is fixed to metal pegs or vine eyes which are driven into the wall and the climbers attach themselves easily to it. Galvanised wire netting is just as suitable, but looks less attractive and is more difficult to cut to size. Netting made out of cord of any kind is short lived and liable to collapse. Few occupations are more frustrating than trying to replace a climber whose support has given away.

We decided that climbers liked a cool and shady root run, so it is clear that the south-facing walls are the least liable to be suitable for climbers. Of course if you feel that you must have a climber on your south wall, it is possible to overcome the difficulty by laying paving slabs, after you have planted your climbers. These will keep the ground cooler than it would be without them and will also stop too rapid evaporation. However as it is possible to grow many attractive half-hardy shrubs against the south wall, it is probably better to use it for this purpose. Wall shrubs have to be tied in and possibly pruned, but they have great attraction and are worth the extra trouble. If it comes to that, climbers are not completely trouble-free when grown against walls; if you are growing them in a hedge or among shrubs or trees, they can usually be left to their own devices, but on a wall they will need pruning in many cases and training.

We have been speaking up to date entirely about shrubby climbers, but we must not forget that there are quite a few that are herbaceous and some that are only annual. No one who has seen *Tropaeolum speciosum* rambling through a Yew hedge will need any further recommendation, but this dies down every autumn to reappear in the spring. In the same way the annual Morning Glory (*Pharbitis tricolor*) is one of the most attractive of annuals.

These herbaceous perennial and annual climbers will thrive in warmer and brighter situations than the shrubby types. By the time that they start to emerge, the surrounding vegetation will be on the move and will provide sufficient shade on their own account. Also they have to make their growth quickly and will therefore want to get as soon as possible out of the shade into the sunlight. As we shall see when we come to consider the plants individually, many of these require to be started in heat and there is really no need to give them a shady situation that would be essential for a perennial climber. Indeed many of them, such as the Morning Glory will only thrive in a warm sunny situation. It will be seen, therefore, that annual climbers require different treatment from all the shrubby types and also from some of the herbaceous climbers. Plants such as *Tropaeolum speciosum* require a cool moist root run, while the Everlasting Pea or *Convolvulus tenuissimus* seem quite indifferent as to position, although the Convolvulus, being a Mediterranean plant, will prefer a sunny situation.

Although, in my opinion, the walls of the house are not the most suitable situation for climbers, there is a lot to be said for using the more vigorous plants to cover sheds and outhouses. These are usually not very attractive, even if not actually unsightly, and will usually be most suitable hosts for climbers. Some climbers, notably ivies, can be trained against wooden fences and will continue to act as a hedge, even after the original wooden fence has disintegrated.

In the early years of the century landscape gardeners used to erect pergolas up which climbers would be trained. These were a series of wooden or metal arches which would be joined by chains or wooden beams; climbers would be trained over the arches and along the longitudinal chains to give a flowered-covered walk. The conception was delightful, but it did not always work out so satisfactorily in practice. The climbers were liable to play host to earwigs and other unwelcome insects and the training of the various plants rather implied the presence of hired labour in abundance. Few of us nowadays have the time to maintain a long pergola walk, but there is no objection to putting up a single arch or even more if you have the time and like the idea. Some of the pergolas had brick columns and wooden beams as cross-bars and these would have the advantage of permanency, although the brickwork would need to be garnished with some support, in the same way as the house walls. The pergola was originally used in Italian gardens where shady walks were an essential and it is not really suited to the British climate.

Once you have got one climber growing really well, there is nothing to stop you growing a second climber up the original.

There is indeed a lot to be said in favour of this course of action as, if you choose the plants carefully, you will have two seasons of flowering. Your second climber should be less vigorous than the plant over which it is to scramble, otherwise you may find that the more vigorous plant will smother its host. For example you can grow a Clematis up a Wisteria, but you cannot grow a Wisteria up a Clematis.

If you are growing climbers on the house walls or up special erections such as pergolas, you will need to spend time in pruning the plants and controlling their growth by tying them in. If the climbers are growing in trees or shrubs they can be left more or less to their own devices. No form of gardening is trouble free and you may have to cut out dead wood or discourage a climber from leaving the host that you have selected in favour of another. Of course if you use the house walls for wall shrubs, which is what I would advise, you can reckon on considerably more trouble in tying in the plants and preventing them from growing in directions that are unsuitable, but on the other hand you will be able to grow plants that you could not otherwise do. It is arguable that Wisteria looks better growing over a house than it does clambering through a tree, but with this possible exception I would say that perennial climbers look better and are certainly more trouble free, when allowed to ascend through shrubs and trees. Another possible exception is the climbing sport of Hybrid Tea or Floribunda rose. These have to be tied in to the wall by means of leather or other ties attached to nails or staples, but they do, in many cases, look better in these positions. In any case this is all a matter of taste and your opinions may be quite different. Sometimes, too, you will have no choice. If you wish to grow a self-supporter like *Hydrangea petiolaris* and do not have a large tree in the garden, you have to make use of the walls.

Planting is a process that should not be hurried. It is best if the climber gets away quickly and makes vigorous growth the first year and this is best done by giving the plant really rich soil in which to make its new roots. It is worthwhile, therefore, to break up the soil to a depth of some 20 in. and incorporate in the soil, compost, or peat, or chopped turves. If you are planting the climber near a tree or shrub and find that the soil is infested with roots, it is an excellent idea to make a wooden frame a yard square and 18 in. deep and bury this. This frame should not have any bottom, but it will effectively keep out marauding roots and let the climber enjoy its soil without more vigorous rivals taking the available nourishment. The roots will eventually descend below the level of the wood and this wood will in time rot away. You do not want to make this box of any very thick timber; its only purpose is to provide a temporary haven while the climber gets established. If it were too solid, it might well make the plant root-bound and prevent vigorous growth.

It is best to put your climbers on the north side of the host tree or shrub. This is the coolest and moistest position. The climber will scramble up and make its way through the host to the south side, where it will produce its flowers. If you have no compass, you can usually see which is the right side to put your climber, by noting the presence of moss or algae which grow on the moister side of the tree. Although the climber will naturally make for the sunniest position for its flowering, it will also spread out and send branches to the east and west. However, it is possible to get climbers to flower on a north-facing wall (provided that it is not too heavily shaded), but climbers will not willingly flower on the north side of shrubs or trees.

When selecting climbers for shrubs or trees it seems best to me to choose climbers that will make their display at a different time to that of the host. This is not essential as one can obviously get very pleasing combinations of colours by selecting two plants that will flower simultaneously, but I think you get more pleasure by having two seasons of beauty. In my garden there is an old apple tree up which I have trained a *Clematis montana rubens*. In some years the Clematis and the apple blossom come out together, which seems a waste to me and I have never thought very highly of my idea. One of the later flowering Clematis, such as *C. tangutica* or *orientalis* would have been far more suitable.

If a tree is to be the host for your climber, you can plant very close to the trunk, without any risk of the ground being infested with roots. By the time the tree is fairly sizeable, it will have sent out its roots to a large radius and the soil immediately around the trunk will not be being used by the tree. There may well be large roots present, which will have to be avoided when digging your hole. But these roots are only taking in nourishment from the soil at their extremities and the portions round the trunk are only transmitting the nutrients to the rest of the tree.

Shrubs, on the other hand, tend to have their roots close to their stems and it is best to put your climber some little way away. It is then tied to a stick inserted at an angle and led along this into the shrub. In very windy districts there is always a risk that this portion of the climber may snap off if it is not supported, so it is then necessary to retain your stick for some years after the climber is supporting itself quite happily in the shrub. By this time the basal stem has become quite thick and will withstand any wind. I have found that Clematis are particularly liable to this wind damage when young.

As we have seen climbers in their natural state are mulched by the leaves falling from their hosts, so if you keep a tidy garden and clear up all the fallen leaves, give your climbers a mulch of some kind. Compost is excellent, but is not always available, nor is animal manure. Peat is quite adequate, so long as it is moistened as soon as it is applied, and treated sewage sludge has much to be said for it. This latter may with advantage be combined with peat. Grass mowings are possible, provided that you have not been treating the lawn with hormone herbicides, but they always seem to bring a lot of weed seed in their train and they must not be used too thickly, otherwise too much heat is generated. Once your climber is doing well there is a very natural tendency to think that mulching is no longer necessary. This may well be true for a year or so, but after that time you might see the climber deteriorating. It depends a good deal on the soil in your garden. If you are one of those fortunate people with a good fat loam, containing ample humus, it is probably unnecessary to do much in the way of mulching; the only essential is to see that the soil does not become dried out during one of our rare hot, dry summers (although cold, windy ones dry out the soil just as much). If the soil is thin and sandy, or thin and chalky, you must give rather copious and bulky mulches. You will have incorporated as much compost as you have been able to obtain when planting your climbers, but this will have to be reinforced yearly. If the soil is of clay, peat is the best material both to mix with the planting soil and to use as a mulch. Peat seems to make the clay somewhat less cohesive and easier to work. Although it is sterile its physical properties are such that it encourages root growth. The ideal and most natural mulch for all climbers is leaf mould and if this is obtainable it is to be preferred.

The question of when to plant your climbers depends to a large extent on where you live. If it is in a district with a history of mild springs with ample rainfall, spring planting is probably the most satisfactory as the plant will at once start to grow. If, on the other hand, you live, as I do, in a district where the spring is usually dry and windy, you will do better to plant in the autumn. In any case evergreens are almost invariably the better for being planted in the autumn, as they continue to make some root growth even during the winter and start far earlier in the spring, although this may be inadvisable in very cold areas. Autumn-planted climbers that may be regarded as tender should be protected as far as possible. The growth is generally somewhat curtailed after planting and the resultant plants are consequently not very large, so it is easy to arrange some form of covering, whether it be sacking, or straw, or polythene sheeting. Ideally this should only be applied when severe weather is expected and should be removed as soon as conditions become milder, even though it may be necessary to replace the protection again subsequently. This is not always convenient in practice and little harm will accrue if the plant is covered from mid-December until mid-March. In the event of severe weather coming earlier or persisting later the protection must obviously be applied according to the weather and not according to the calendar. With really tender subjects it may be necessary to apply some form of protection every winter, but it will only be possible to protect the base of the climber. Although this will break afresh, it is not worth your while to keep any plant, however beautiful, that is going to be repeatedly checked in this manner. If you live in a district with a tradition of severe winters, these tender climbers should not be attempted. However there are occasions where the winters are usually mild, but occasionally, as in 1962–3, severe weather is experienced. Under these exceptional circumstances, protection will save the plant to make a new framework. Although many climbers are described as being tender, they will often be found growing in districts that might appear to be highly unsuitable, and there are often situations in a garden that may well be milder than positions only a few yards away. There is a lot to be said for being adventurous. It is frustrating to lose a plant, but the man who makes no mistakes is unlikely to make a very interesting garden. Hardiness usually seems to be a dominant character, so that if you can get seeds of unusually hardy forms of reputedly tender climbers, there is the probability that these seedlings will also prove exceptionally hardy. If you can obtain cuttings, these will be even more satisfactory.

When planting your climbers, it is advisable to spread the roots out rather than to leave them all bunched together. In the cases of plants such as clematis, which are always supplied in pots, it is only necessary to unravel gently the tangle of roots at the bottom of the pot. Clematis resent any disturbance or damage to the roots, so they should be interfered with as little as possible; on the other hand if the roots are in a thick tangle they will grow away better after being disentangled. It is, like almost all gardening operations, a matter of common sense. Now that many plants are grown in containers for sale at garden centres, it is possible to purchase them and plant them at any time that is convenient to you. Personally I have found that it is by no means easy to remove a large root-ball from half an oil drum without damaging the roots and I would always recommend starting with comparatively small plants, rather than with large specimens. If you purchase plants in containers in mid-summer, you must take great care to see that the plant does not dry out during the period when it is rooting into the garden soil and this will entail a lot of work that planting at the usual time, be it autumn or spring, will not require. Sometimes there are compensating advantages for this extra trouble; you may wish to get a climber established before the autumn, but by and large you will find that planting at the conventional times is the most trouble free method.

When putting any plant in the soil it is essential to get the soil in close contact with the root-ball, but on the other hand you do not want to impact the soil too much. If your soil is not too wet when planting, an excellent method is to half fill your hole with soil which is lightly firmed down and is then well watered. The next day you can fill the hole up and water again. This will settle the soil very effectively. However in autumn and spring the soil is usually fairly well soaked and, if it is at all heavy, this method will not be very practical. Under these circumstances it is best to tread the soil in, but do this operation rather gently. Do not stamp the soil down, but firm it lightly with your feet.

Most climbers benefit by being cut back after planting. I would be a little chary of doing this with evergreens, particularly with *Clematis armandii*, which resents disturbance in any way and is liable to die out of sheer temper, but all deciduous climbers can be cut back with advantage when being planted, with a very few exceptions. The amount that you cut off will depend on the plant itself, but with most climbers you can reckon on cutting off half the current growth. With the large-flowered Clematis it may well be two-thirds of the current growth that is cut away, while with roses one third will probably be sufficient. Whether this pruning back is done when you plant the climbers in the autumn or is deferred until the beginning of spring is a matter of choice. All Vitis species will have to be pruned in late autumn, as at any other period there is a risk of excessive bleeding of sap. Cutting back in the autumn certainly obviates the risk of wind damage, but, on the other hand, if severe frosts are experienced it may be found that some of the tips have been killed, so that there is little live wood left in the spring. This is not necessarily a bad thing; two leads are usually quite sufficient in the first year, but if the amount of dormant buds is restricted, it means that any damage by slugs or normal carelessness may be serious. My own practice is to shorten the growths slightly when planting in the autumn and prune a second time at the end of the winter.

When selecting your climbers you will want to bear in mind their ultimate dimensions. These will be given when the plants are discussed individually, but it must be borne in mind that these dimensions are what are most likely to be met with, and can on occasion be exceeded or not attained. They will give you a rough guide as to the dimensions that they will reach, but it is only a rough guide. You may get a better impression by seeing how these plants flourish in your neighbourhood. The local climate can make so much difference to plants of all kinds and climbers are no exception. The last few paragraphs have been concerned with shrubby climbers. Naturally you cannot cut back herbaceous or annual climbers.

Herbaceous climbers are certainly best planted in the autumn, as by the time that spring planting is possible, they will have begun to make the current year's shoots and these can easily be damaged. Slugs may well be your greatest enemy with these subjects and it is advisable to scatter slug pellets around the place where the shoots should emerge. It is even more effective to make a circle of perforated zinc round the plant. Slugs, for some reason, cannot walk on zinc and this is an effective and not very unsightly method of preserving your plants from these fiends. Perforated zinc can be obtained from builders' merchants and they will probably be prepared to cut it into strips for you. These should ideally be about 10 in. wide, so that you bury 5 in. and leave 5 in. protruding. Once the plants are well established they can probably dispense with this protection and it can be moved to plants that require it more. I would personally keep it round the plants for the first two winters; after this the plant will be able to produce more shoots if those first produced are damaged. Such a scheme is practicable for most plants, but will scarcely serve for more than one year with *Tropaeolum speciosum*, as this tends to travel underground and may well come up in the second year outside its protecting zinc. In any case, as we shall see, this plant requires special treatment at all times, prior to its establishment.

The dimensions of annual climbers depend far more on climate and treatment than do those of perennials. If the soil is well prepared and if watering is assiduously attended to, they will make much larger plants than if put into the soil and left to take pot luck Moreover a hot summer will generally result in far larger plants, unless their growth is restricted through drought. We cannot control the weather, but we can control the soil and the water supply, so that the dimensions of our annual climbers depends to a large extent on our own exertions.

These general remarks are already being diminished by the mention of exceptions. It will probably be best to bring them to a close and to start considering the plants individually.

2 No visible means of support

The plants to be discussed in this chapter are those that scramble through and over shrubs and trees in the wild state. They start by throwing up fairly rigid stems, but these elongate rapidly and do not noticeably thicken at the base, so that they soon become top-heavy. In the right position they have ascended among tree and shrub branches before this happens, and use these branches as a support for further ascent. Perhaps the most notable of the plants in this section are the climbing roses and these have their branches armed with very large spines. These help to keep the branches anchored among their hosts, but it would not be accurate to say that they climb by means of their thorns, as is sometimes stated. Such plants are best grown in the way that nature has supplied for them. If they are grown on a wall or on a fence they have to be tied in at frequent intervals. It is no good giving them a framework of wire netting and expecting them to support themselves. However two of the plants in this section are only half-hardy and must have wall protection in all but the warmest parts of Devon and Cornwall, the west coast of Scotland and parts of Ireland. The Abutilon is a comparatively small shrub and it is not much trouble to tie it in, but Berberidopsis is fairly vigorous and quite a lot of work is entailed in growing it. It is perhaps simpler to grow this up another climber or through a wall shrub.

If these plants are placed where no ascent into trees or shrubs is possible, they will trail along the ground, and in some cases may provide quite adequate ground cover. Plants such as the Winter Jasmine and some of the less vigorous roses make a satisfactory display if they can fall down a bank or over some low wall. However, if it is possible, it is much more satisfactory to grow these through a tree or a bush. Even so it may be necessary to give a little support in the early stages. This may be done either by means of tying the new shoots to a cane and leading them up this into the host or else by tying them directly on to the host. This latter method is best with the very vigorous *Synstylae* roses, which only need the slightest of supports. It should be borne in mind that the new growths are very brittle, so they should not be subjected to any great force, just lightly supported. Let us now consider the plants in more detail; they are listed in alphabetical order, rather than in any order of merit, on which opinions could differ.

ABUTILON

Abutilon is a member of the mallow family and none of its members are hardy except in the most sheltered counties.

Abutilon megapotamicum This is a very slender shrub, whose branches require some support. It seldom exceeds a height of 6 ft out of doors, but will go somewhat higher in a cool greenhouse. It is best placed on a south or west facing wall or wooden fence. If it is to be planted against the house wall, it is worth recollecting that the foundations probably continue for some 12 in. from the wall that is visible and that all wall plants are best planted about 2 ft from the wall, or even further if that is convenient. *A. megapotamicum* is a native of Brazil, albeit from high regions, and flowers nearly continuously under glass. In the open it generally starts flowering in late April and continues until the autumn frosts. It is evergreen with rather elongated heart-shaped leaves about 3 in. long and with flowers hanging from the upper leaf axils. These flowers are surrounded by a nearly scarlet calyx, which contrasts well with the yellow petals. The flower is bell-shaped and the calyx and petals together reach a length of 3 in. Once established, the plant will withstand severe frosts, but it is a plant that is best planted in the spring, when the risk of frost has gone. There is a form with variegated leaves, they are blotched with yellow, which is considerably less vigorous and, to my eyes, the variegation is not very handsome. I have not heard of seed being produced in this country and propagation is by means of hard wood cuttings. These are usually taken in early spring, but need a temperature around 70°F to root.

A. × milleri This is a hybrid between *A. megapotamicum* and the rather stout *A. pictum*. This latter plant needs greenhouse protection and so the hybrid is less hardy than *A. megapotamicum*. It has the same slender habit, but lacks the brilliant sepals. The flowers are yellow streaked with red. Although an attractive plant, it does not seem to me to have any advantages over its hardier parent. It will, however, grow considerably taller.

BERBERIDOPSIS

There is only one species in this genus, *B. corallina*. This is a native of Chile and like most importations from that country needs rather special treatment. It requires an acid soil, which is cool and moist, and needs a fairly shady situation. Most of the spectacular Chilean climbers, all on the borderline of hardiness, come from rain forests and appreciate a constantly moist atmosphere. In mild climates they can be grown on north facing walls, but where it is less equable, they will do better on a west wall. If a south wall is shaded it could be grown on that, but the exposed south wall would be too hot and dry. In those parts of the country that feel the benefit of the Gulf Stream, it can be grown through shrubs as nature intended. In very cold districts it should not be attempted and much of eastern and south eastern England is liable to be too dry, although it grows well in parts of Sussex.

The plant is not a very rapid grower and it may be necessary to wait a few years before any flowers are produced. Berberidopsis has oblong heart-shaped evergreen leaves about 3 in. long. They are edged with prickles and their supposed resemblance to Berberis leaves have given the plant its name, (it belongs to the Flacourtiaceae). The flowers resemble ruby-red berries and are produced in racemes at the ends of the branches. The flowers appear from July onwards, sometimes lasting until September and are thus the more to be prized for appearing at a season when few climbers, other than some Clematis, are in flower. If it is grown on a wall there is a lot to be said for growing it either up another climber or through a wall shrub, as the lower portions of the plant become bare and leafless when the plant is mature and look unattractive. If seed is set, this is the best method of propagation, but it is possible to take cuttings in the spring or to layer growths as they emerge from the root. This is usually done in the autumn.

CESTRUM

Cestrum is a genus of solanaceous shrubs from Central and South America; They are not reliably hardy, but will often survive on sheltered walls for some time, particularly in such places as the Isle of Wight and Cornwall. They seldom exceed 8 ft in height and might well prove satisfactory in comparatively cool districts, if care was taken to protect the base of the plant against severe frost. The hardiest, *C. parqui*, is slightly more vigorous than the other species, but is not one of the most attractive. It has rather small yellowish flowers in a terminal panicle. On the other hand they have a pleasant fragrance at night. *C. aurantiacum* has bright orange flowers, while, *C. fasciculatum*, *C.×newellii* and *C. purpureum* have carmine or reddish-purple flowers and are evergreen. In *C. purpureum* the inflorescences hang down, while they are erect in the other species. They all have a long flowering season and are very suitable for training on walls, provided climatic conditions allow. The flowers are generally borne on the top of the current year's growth, so that even if cut down by frost, they may well produce flowers in the summer. They are easily propagated by cuttings of half-ripened wood, so that, if greenhouse accommodation is available, there is no difficulty in keeping your stock going. Although they are usually only found in the warmer counties, there is always the chance that they may survive in places that would seem unpromising. At one time the species with orange and crimson flowers were put in the genus *Habrothamnus*, but that has now been suppressed.

CLEMATIS

The Majority of Clematis climb by means of twisting the petioles around their host and will be found in chapter 4. There are, however, three hybrids of climbing Clematis with herbaceous species and they should be described here.

Clematis × durandii This hybrid was formed by pollinating the herbaceous *C. integrifolia* with *C.×jackmannii. C. integrifolia* is an attractive herbaceous species, with nodding bell-shaped blue flowers, while *C. jackmannii* is the common large-flowered violet Clematis; the most well-known of the large-flowered hybrids. This throws up long stems, sometimes reaching a height of 10 ft and has simple leaves, unlike the compound ones of most Clematis. The violet flowers are intermediate between the bell-shape of *C. integrifolia* and the flat open flowers of the large-flowered hybrids. The stems are slightly woody and may persist from year to year, but fresh stems will eventually replace them.

Clematis × hendersonii (also known as *eriostemon* and *intermedia*). This is one of the earliest clematis hybrids, dating from 1830, when it appeared in the nursery of Messrs Henderson. The parentage is *C. integrifolia* pollinated by *C. viticella.* This latter species is a climber with myriads of small pendulous violet flowers in late summer. The hybrid is herbaceous; the stems being of only annual duration. They reach, however, up to 6 or 8 ft and so must be tied in to some support. The flowers themselves are very similar to those of *C. integrifolia*, but have the advantage of being fragrant and are displayed to better advantage. They appear from July onwards and always attract attention through their unusual shape and good blue colour. It is irritating having to tie the growths in, but the plant is so attractive that it is worth the slight trouble involved.

Clematis × jouiniana The seed parent here is *C. heracleifolia* var. *davidiana*. This is a plant with a woody base and herbaceous stems, bearing heads of pale blue hyacinth-like flowers in the autumn. The pollen parent is our native Travellers' Joy, *C. vitalba*. The resultant plant is a vigorous climber, that can exceed 12 ft in height. The stems are only partly woody and die back to about half their length in the winter. The small, starry flowers are produced in a terminal panicle and are the palest mauve, fading to white. The main advantage of the plant is its late flowering, from August until October. It is not nearly distinguished enough to be given wall space and is perhaps best planted in a hedge, through which it can scramble. It could be trained along a fence or railings, but there are many better plants for this purpose. On the other hand it looks attractive peeping out from holly or some other dark evergreen and in these situations it can be left to itself to scramble through the twigs and branches.

JASMINUM

Most of the jasmines are twining climbers and will appear in chapter V, but there are two species that come into the present category.

Jasminum nudiflorum This, the Winter Jasmine, is really a very lax shrub and has no real right to get into this book at all. However it is grown so frequently as a climber that it would be wrong to exclude it. In any case it will make an agreeable display if allowed to grow through some shrub and it can be trained against walls or fences, where it may reach a height of 12 ft. Normally it will not much exceed 6 ft in height. I suppose that this is one of the most valuable of all garden shrubs, flowering, as it does, through the dreariest of the winter months, from November to March. The severest frosts do not seem to touch it; although any flowers that may be out when the frost comes are destroyed, the unopened buds will start to emerge as soon as the frost is past. The plant also seems to be completely indifferent as far as soil and aspect are concerned. It will flower happily on a north wall. If trained against a wall, it will fountain out, so that ample space should be provided; if the wall is too near a path, it is liable to encroach and be rather a nuisance. I am not sure why it is regarded as necessary to grow it against a wall. I imagine the earlier gardeners thought that a plant that flowered throughout the winter must need some protection, but there seems no reason why it should not be grown among shrubs, either as a spreading shrub in its own right or leaning over another. The flowers are produced on the current year's growth, so that if it is used as a wall shrub, it may be pruned hard back in the spring. The main shoots do not want interference, but all lateral growths should be cut back to two or three buds. This will encourage vigorous growth of the flower-bearing laterals.

Jasminum primulinum This is one of several plants imported from Chinese gardens that have never been found in the wild. It resembles a giant *J. nudiflorum* with flowers 2 in. across of a rather softer yellow than the Winter Jasmine. It can reach a height of 15 ft, but is only possible out of doors in the mildest localities and even in these may suffer in exceptional winters. The flowers come in the spring after *J. nudiflorum* has finished blooming. There do not seem to be many hybrid jasmines known, but if it were possible to cross these two species and get a plant with the hardiness of *J. nudiflorum* and flowers the size of *J. primulinum*, the breeder would have achieved a very remarkable shrub.

ROSA

The climbing roses form the most important section of this chapter and are so heterogeneous a group, that it is not easy to devise a method of treating them compactly and satisfactorily. Since Graham Thomas was easily able to devote a complete book to the subject (*Climbing Roses, Old and New*, Phoenix House, 1965) it is evident that some abridgement is necessary here. What I propose to do is to describe the various climbing species, but when we come to the hybrid races, I shall make no attempt to enumerate the various and numerous cultivars. These are generally well described in most catalogues and are very fully described in Graham Thomas's book.

The section of the great Rose family that most consistently gives rise to climbing roses is the *Synstylae*. The section gets its name from the fact that the styles are united in a column, whereas in most roses they are spread out. There are only two species in the section that do not normally climb. These are *R. soulieana*, which is a very vigorous shrub and *R. wichuraiana*, a parent of many climbing roses, but which itself prefers to creep along the ground. In fact it makes a quite admirable ground cover. The stems root in the ground as they elongate, the plate is, rather unusually among roses, evergreen, and it flowers as late as August. It can be used as a climber, but its natural habit is a creeper.

Most of this section which are grown in gardens are very vigorous climbers reaching at least 25 ft high and some capable of reaching 40 ft. They are best trained into mature trees, although in the Savill Gardens 'Wedding Day', a *R. sinowilsonii* hybrid, looks very effective trained along the top of a long wooden fence. If trained up trees, they should be planted on the north side and the new shoots should be very lightly supported until they have reached a sufficient height for the tree branches to support them. The new growths are brittle and not very flexible, so care should be taken that they are not damaged. Once they are in the tree they can be left to themselves. The species most commonly met with are *Rr. brunonii*, *filipes*, *helenae*, *longicuspis*, *rubus* and *sinowilsonii*, to this list might be added Sir Frederick's Stern's *R. sinowilsonii* hybrid known as 'Wedding Day'. Of these the most vigorous are *brunonii*, *filipes*, *rubus* and *sinowilsonii*.

They all have enormous panicles of medium-sized single white flowers at varying times from June to July. *R. sinowilsonii* is rather tender and is not suitable for most gardens. It has leaves up to a foot long which are purple underneath and the young growths and thorns are of a shining mahogany colour. It is handsomer in its foliage than any other rose of the section. Other matters being equal, the best of the group are *R. helenae* and *R. rubus*. *R. helenae* flowers towards the end of June and the flowers are followed by panicles of scarlet heps, which are not found in other members of this section, and which transform the plant in autumn with a most wonderful display of what looks from the ground like thousands of wild strawberries. *R. rubus* is, with *R. longicuspis*, the last of this group to flower and is somewhat richer in colour. The flowers are pinkish in the bud and open to a cream, rather than a white, and have an orange stain at their base. All these roses are intensely fragrant and can perfume the whole garden when they are in flower. 'Wedding Day' has yellowish buds, which open cream and fade to white. Unfortunately as the flowers age they tend to get blotched with muddy pink and look less attractive.

None of these roses will flower until they have made ample growth and you must expect to wait two or three years after planting them, before you are greeted with their overwhelming display of blossom. *R. brunonii* is sometimes affected in very severe winters, but, in my experience, once it is well established, the damage is far less than most books suggest.

The Musk Rose, *R. moschata*, was very highly prized in former days for its late flowering. The blooms appear in August and September and have a very characteristic perfume. The plant is reasonably compact, not exceeding 12 ft in height, and has been rescued from extinction in this country at the last moment by Graham Thomas. This is a valuable rose for its late flowering and remarkable fragrance.

Rosa multiflora, an ancestor of many of the old Rambler Roses, can be left without support to form a jungle. As such it is used along many American highways as a buffer against any cars that may leave the road. It will grow up to 20 ft if trained in a tree. The type plant has white flowers, but there are many putative hybrids that were imported from Japan in the early 19th century with double and semi-double pink flowers; the most well-known of these is the 'Seven Sisters Rose'. These forms of *R. multiflora* flower in July and have an agreeable fragrance. They are followed by decorative small red heps. They are not among the most distinguished in this section, but frequently appear in old gardens, where they have been used as an understock.

Rosa arvensis, the Ayrshire Rose, is an inhabitant of our own hedgerows. During the early nineteenth century it was used as a parent of climbing roses and one, 'Splendens', still survives on account of its perfume, which is said to resemble myrrh. This grows to 15 ft and has semi-double flowers, which appear to be rosy-purple in bud, but which open a pale cream.

Along the Mediterranean you may find the evergreen *R. sempervirens*. This is not very distinguished in itself, but has served as the parent for two hybrids raised in 1826 and 1827 by the gardener to the Duc d'Orléans, a M. Jacques. 'Adelaide d'Orléans' has hanging corymbs of semi-double pale pink flowers, while 'Félicité et Perpétue' has pure white flowers that emerge from crimson-flushed buds. Both these hybrids will retain some of their leaves throughout the year and neither are excessively vigorous, although 'Adelaide d'Orléans' can reach 15 ft. The other hybrid seldom exceeds 12 ft. Both flower towards the end of June.

In the U.S.A. the *Synstylae* are represented by the Prairie Rose, *R. setigera*. This tends to be a sprawling shrub, rather than a climber, although, since it bears shoots 12 ft long, it can be used as a climber. The single fragrant pink flowers are rather muddy in colour, but come quite late in the season and so are useful on that account. There are said to be other colour forms in the wild and fresh collecting might bring some useful variants. This is an exceptionally hardy rose, used to tolerating temperatures far lower than anything we are liable to experience. It was therefore used as a parent for a race of 'Prairie Roses', none of which are apparently sufficiently distingushed to have been imported by British nurserymen and so they are not known over here.

The Asian members of this group, *R. brunonii*, *R. helenae*, etc., show even more variability when raised from seed than most roses do and, as a result, some are known by clonal names. Thus, for example, the best form of *R. filipes* is known as 'Kiftsgate', and the best form of *R. brunonii* is that called 'La Mortola'. The clonal names in each case refer to the gardens whence they originated.

When the plants are received, they should be lightly pruned and after that little further pruning is necessary, or, indeed, possible. In theory old branches should be cut out, when there are sufficient fresh shoots to replace them, but this is seldom practicable and they may be regarded as trouble free.

The other groups of roses contain few climbers. The section known as *Banksianae* is confined to two species, only one of which is in cultivation; This is Lady Banks's Rose, *Rosa banksiae*, brought from China by William Kerr in 1807. This is a very attractive rose, that must, however, have the protection of a south wall. It seems to tolerate a certain amount of frost, so that it may be seen growing in relatively ungenial districts, but it needs plenty of sun to ripen its wood. The flowers are produced on laterals springing from the old wood and pruning is practically minimal. The first importation was a double white form and was shortly followed by the double yellow, which has proved the easiest to cultivate in this country. Unfortunately it has far less of the violet-like fragrance of the white forms. The single yellow and white are comparatively recent introductions to western gardens and are very difficult to obtain. The flowers are small but produced in great quantity and very early in the season; usually it is in flower by the end of May. It is not a very rapid grower, but will eventually make a large plant, sometimes reaching a height of 20 ft with a similar spread. In warmer climes they can grow it in trees where it looks exquisite, but that is not possible in Great Britain, not even in the Channel Islands.

Slightly less tender, but still requiring wall protection is the Macartney Rose, *R. bracteata*. This is evergreen and the leaves are in themselves extremely handsome and so are the flower buds with their large leafy bracts. The white flowers, single and about 3 in. across, are produced from the end of June until the autumn, so that they give a good period of display. It seldom exceeds 12 ft in height, although it has been known to go higher in favourable situations. At one time a number of hybrids were known, but the only one that appears to survive is 'Mermaid'. This is a splendid rose with large single pale yellow flowers. It is far hardier then *R. bracteata*, but can be damaged in severe winters. In mild districts is it evergreen, but elsewhere it is deciduous. It was bred by crossing *R. bracteata* with a yellow Hybrid Tea and was introduced in 1918. It does not start to flower until July, but continues until the frosts come. Although it can, in theory, reach a height of 25 ft, it is not usually more than half this height.

Another rather tender climber is the Cherokee Rose, *R. laevigata*. Although a native of China, it has become so naturalized in parts of the U.S.A. that it has become the State Flower of Georgia. It can easily be distinguished from all other roses, by the fact that the leaf is composed of only three leaflets which are glossy and make a rather brilliant display. The large single white flowers appear at the end of May, but once the display is over, there is nothing more to look forward to. As it makes a large plant capable of reaching a height of 20 ft, it is very seldom seen in this country. There are, however, a couple of hybrids which are in some ways more attractive, are far more reliably hardy and are comparatively restrained growers. One is the rose sometimes known as 'Anemonoides' and sometimes as *R. sinica* (a synonym of *R. laevigata*) 'Anemone'. This is, in my opinion, one of the most attractive of all roses. It has large single flowers of soft clear pink veined with a deeper crimson. It is one of the first roses to appear, sometimes showing a few flowers by the end of April in a mild season and making its main display from mid-May over three or four weeks. It is thought to have been bred by crossing *R. laevigata* with a Tea Rose. In 1913 a sport of this appeared with bright crimson flowers and was given the name 'Ramona'. It is not, perhaps, quite so attractive as 'Anemonoides' but is again among the most attractive roses. Both of these do best against a wall, although it need not necessarily be a south-facing one and need little pruning apart from cutting out the dead wood, of which there is usually rather more than in the case of other climbing roses.

The last of the climbing species belongs, like the China Rose (which is a climber in its usual wild state, but is not in cultivation), to the section *Indicae*. This is the Tea Rose, *R. gigantea*. This is practically impossible in this country. There are records of it surviving for some years in various parts of the country, but they do not seem to do it for long. A severe frost, such as we had in 1962–3 will cut it to the ground, although it may re-emerge. Usually our summers are not hot enough to ripen the new growth. This is a pity, as it is a superb plant with lemon yellow drooping flowers with the characteristic tea scent. In the wild it can reach a height of 40 ft, so it is scarcely a plant for the small garden in any case. There are however two hybrids, presumably with Hybrid Teas, which are possible, although they need a lot of space. These are 'Belle Portugaise' which is so impressive at Wisley and 'La Follette'. 'Belle Portugaise' has salmon pink flowers, while 'La Follette' is deeper and has a copper-coloured reverse to the petals. Both of these require a sheltered position and at least 20 ft of wall, although they do not spread so much as their height would suggest. They flower in June and give a really superlative display after a hot summer. However this is not of very long duration and it is best to grow a second and later flowering climber up these *R. gigantea* hybrids, as otherwise they are scarcely worth the space they take up. In any case they are not suitable for cold localities and one can probably do better with the available wall space. In warmer climes they are superlative.

Rambler Roses are chiefly based on *R. wichuraiana*, but *R. multiflora* certainly enters into some, such as the once popular 'Crimson Rambler'. They are characterized by huge panicles of coloured flowers, generally in late July and early August they flower consistently on the second year wood and are the only climbing roses to need constant pruning. This is simply done when the flowering is over, and consists of cutting out the shoots that have flowered and, if the rose is trained to some structure, tying in the new shoots that have appeared during the current year. The old favourites such as 'Dorothy Perkins' and 'Crimson Rambler' are very susceptible to mildew and have been replaced by the similar 'Debutante' and 'Crimson Shower'. 'Debutante' has the advantage of being perfumed. There are two ramblers of similar parentage (*moschata* × *multiflora*), 'Madame d'Arblay' in which *R. multiflora* was the seed parent, and 'The Garland' where it was the pollen parent, both of which are noteworthy for their fragrance and floriferousness. The flowers open a pale pink and fade quickly to white. These look particularly attractive when growing through evergreens, such as Yew or Chamaecyparis.

At a later date *R. wichuraiana* was crossed with various H.T. roses and the resultant hybrids are larger flowered than the Ramblers. They include such popular plants as 'Alberic Barbier' and 'Emily Gray'. They are characterized by the glossy leaves of the climbing parent. They have their main flowering season at the end of June, but will generally continue to produce a few flowers until the autumn. These do not need the severe pruning that the Ramblers require, but only the oldest wood should be removed, apart, of course, from any dead wood which should never be left on any rose. All these roses are moderately vigorous, reaching a height of 15–20 ft, while 'La Perle' with very fragrant, white, yellow-centred flowers can reach 30 ft and is very vigorous. They are all very suitable for training along fences or allowed to scramble through a hedge. They are among the pleasantest of climbing hybrids.

The first recurrent flowering roses were raised in Charleston, S. Carolina, and distributed by Louis Noisette in 1819. It was a second generation cross of a recurrent flowering China rose and *R. moschata*. This original cross was raised by a nurseryman called Champneys and was known as 'Champneys' Pink Cluster'. This was not recurrent, but seeds from this plant produced a certain number of recurrent bloomers. They were known, from the raiser's name as Noisette Roses. The original Noisettes were characterized by bunches of rather small flowers, which were very fragrant. Around 1830 they were crossed with a large flowered yellow Tea Rose and not only were yellow flowers introduced to the race, but the flowers began to reach the same size as the Tea Roses themselves. The first plants, some of which still survive, had small double flowers that were produced from mid-June onwards. They are not particularly rampant growers, seldom exceeding 15 ft. As the Tea Rose (which is a hybrid of *R. chinensis* and *R. gigantea*) was repeatedly bred into the Noisettes they became less hardy, although the flowers had by now become as large as the Tea Roses themselves. The earlier ones such as 'Lamarque' and 'Desprez à fleur jaune' are possible against warm walls, but the glory of this section 'Marechal Niel' requires a cool greenhouse. An exception to this prevailing tenderness is the still popular 'Gloire de Dijon' which was introduced as long ago as 1853, but is still grown to a large extent.

The Climbing Sports of the H.T. roses are very attractive, but seldom have more than the one display of flowers. There are however one or two exceptions such as 'High Noon' and 'New Dawn'. Most of them are known as bush roses, but often the climbing sport has survived, when the bush has been superseded. Thus it is easy to obtain 'Climbing Lady Hillingdon' or 'Climbing Caroline Testout' while the bush roses would be sought for with difficulty. There are some of these roses such as the nearly black

'Guinée' and the lemon 'Paul's Lemon Pillar' which are only known as climbers. Most of these make fairly vigorous plants reaching from 15 to 20 ft and require little pruning.

The most recent climbers are described as Pillar Roses and flower over the same period as the H.T.s and Floribundas. They should be distinguished from the climbing sports of Floribundas, which usually only have one season of display. They are not very tall growing; the usual height is about 8 ft and I find them singularly frustrating plants, in spite of their handsome flowers. How many of us are going to erect pillars in our gardens in order to grow these roses? They produce so many shoots that they are not really suitable for tying into walls and will probably be best trained against wooden fences. If your garden has no wooden fences I suggest that you will be happier without Pillar Roses. They are not sufficiently vigorous to train through shrubs; or rather they are not sufficiently tall, they are vigorous enough. They might well succeed trained through a fairly low hedge. One does not wish to be without them, since such plants as 'Meg' and 'Parade' are remarkably attractive. They are mostly very thorny and tying them in is an operation that may be painful. Stout gloves are an advantage, although they make you feel remarkably ham-handed. There must be a place in the garden for these delightful flowers, but I am baffled to know where it is.

The Boursault climbers are all thornless and of rather doubtful parentage. The old growers thought that they were crosses between the China Rose and the Alpine Rose, *R. pendulina*. This now seems improbable owing to the chromosome count of the latter species and it is thought that a North American rose, such as *R. foliolosa* may be the parent responsible for the thornlessness. For some reason the most popular of the thornless climbers, 'Zephirine Drouhin' is not usually included among the Boursaults, but it is hard to see where else it will fit in. (It was put originally among the Bourbon roses.) This is one of the most fragrant of all roses and flowers continuously from May until the autumn. The colour is a rather harsh shade of shocking pink, but its more agreeably coloured sport, 'Kathleen Harrop', seems to have lost the fragrance of the original. Another Boursault is 'Madame Sancy de Parabère' which has large flowers of a good soft pink, of a shape that is unique among roses; the outer petals are so much larger than the central ones, that the flower looks like a rose in a saucer. This, like the other surviving Boursaults, is devoid of perfume. The Boursaults are moderately vigorous, 'Zephirine Drouhin' reaches about 10 ft, while the others are nearer 15 ft.

'Zephirine Drouhin' will thrive splendidly rambling through a hedge and so will the others, but these can also scramble through individual shrubs, like many of the other climbers.

We have cantered rather briskly through a vast subject and have had to ignore a few plants that do not fit in happily in any of the categories, into which, for convenience sake, the climbing roses have been divided. Among these is the enchanting 'Climbing Cécile Brunner', which deserves a short note. 'Cécile Brunner' herself, is not easy to fit into any category. She bears heads of flowers, each one with the perfect shape of 'Ophelia' but only about an inch long. She used to be put in the Polyantha section, but the flowers have a perfection of form which is lacking in any other of the old Polyanthas. The climbing sport has slightly larger leaves and flowers than the bush and can reach a height of 20 ft. The pale pink flowers are produced in great profusion and over quite a long period. I rank this very highly indeed among the climbers.

Perhaps we should just recapitulate the treatment for these roses. With the Ramblers, once they are established, it is necessary to cut out the old canes after they have completed their flowering and train in the current year's canes in their place. With the others it is only necessary to cut out the dead wood and some of the old wood, when the plant is becoming overcrowded. The Banksian Roses flower off the older wood and it is only wood that is about 7 years old that should be cut out. The vigorous climbers that ascend high into trees are very rarely pruned at all. It is not possible, even though it might be desirable. Roses are greedy and will appreciate as much food as you can give them and like an annual mulch around the roots.

RUBUS

The various climbing species of Rubus are glorified brambles and are best placed in the wilder parts of the garden. They tend to be well covered with thorns and so are rather tiresome to handle. They are indifferent as to the nature of the soil and seem to give of their best when encouraged to ramble among low-growing shrubs. They can usually be propagated by allowing the tips of the canes to fall to the ground, where they will root.

Rubus bellidiflorus This is more properly called *R. ulmifolius* var. *bellidiflorus*. When not in flower it looks like an ordinary bramble, but this illusion is dispelled as soon as the flowers appear.

They are a soft pink and fully double and continue for some time from late summer into autumn. These flowers are about the same size as the ordinary wild Blackberry, about $\frac{3}{4}$ in. across, but they are produced in large panicles and the plant is really very showy when in flower. At one time there were two other forms of *R. ulmifolius* in cultivation, with large panicles of single rose-pink flowers. These were the var. *inermis* which had the advantage of carrying no prickles and *variegatus*, which had yellow veins to the leaves, which were sufficiently prominent to give a variegated effect.

Some of the other species may not be easy to obtain, and there are some listed which are, to my mind, of little interest. However they are all given a notice here.

R. australis This is a tall climber from New Zealand, which is so heavily armed as to make a completely impenetrable fence, should one be desired. The plant is evergreen and dioecious; that is to say that male and female flowers are borne on different plants. The small white flowers are borne in panicles that may be 2 ft long, so that it is quite attractive in flower. Owing to its fearsome armature this is probably not wanted in many gardens.

R. flagelliflorus This is one of a number of Chinese species, that are not very attractive in flower, but which have a graceful habit and attractive leaves. In this species the evergreen leaves are simple, up to 7 in. long, more or less egg-shaped with a downy underside. The young shoots, which may make 5 ft of growth in the season, are covered with a sort of white felt. The plant has prickles, but they are not excessively savage. The white flowers are inconspicuous and are followed by small edible blackberries.

R. henryi Another evergreen Chinese species, capable of attaining 20 ft and therefore needing a tree or very large shrub as host. The leaves are deeply lobed (or in the var. *bambusarum* trifoliate) from 4–6 in. long with an attractive white felt on the underside. The plant is only slightly prickly. The flowers appear in short racemes, but are of an attractive pink colour and are followed by black fruits.

R. lambertianus Another Chinese species, but only semi-evergreen and, so far as I am concerned, with no very obvious garden qualities.

R. lineatus. This straggling shrub will reach a height of 10 ft, but needs careful placing, as its great attraction is the silvery underside of the leaves. These are large and generally composed of five leaflets. Neither the flowers nor the fruits are very conspicuous. It is a plant of doubtful hardiness in districts away from the west coast. It is practically without prickles, which is an advantage.

R. malifolius. This is one of the few Chinese species that are characterized by handsome flowers. It is deciduous and a scrambler, reaching up to 10 ft in height. The white flowers are an inch across and appear in racemes that are 6 in. long. The leaves are simple and oval in shape, up to 5 in. long.

R. parkeri Another Chinese species, although again this is deciduous, that is grown for its handsome foliage. In this case the leaves are up to 7 in. long, oblong-ovate with wavy margins. They are covered on the underside with reddish-brown down. The stems, which are only slightly prickly, are covered with grey hairs. The white flowers are inconspicuous, but the inflorescence is not unattractive, owing to the red hairs which cover the calices. The stems tend to be of biennial duration, growing the first year and dying at the end of the second after flowering and fruiting. The plant therefore requires similar treatment to that advised for Rambler roses.

R. phoenicolasius The Japanese Wineberry. This is a scrambling shrub very similar to the blackberry in habit. Like the last species it is deciduous and the stems are biennial. The new growths are covered thickly with red bristles which makes them very ornamental and these persist although they are always most notable at the growing tip. The flowers are pink, but minute and completely hidden in the large star-shaped calyx, but the fruits are nearly scarlet and very handsome. Their flavour, however, is insipid.

R. setchuensis (omeiensis) Another deciduous Chinese species described as a very straggling shrub. This has palmate leaves like those of a maple, with very conspicuous stipules at the base of the leaf stalk. The plant has no prickles. The leaves may be 7 in. long and as much across and the inflorescence is quite large, composed of purple flowers ½ in. across. The flowers appear in July and the black fruit, that ripens somewhat late, is said to be well-flavoured.

R. thyrsoideus plenus (linkianus) A double white form of one of our native Blackberries, this is useful for its late flowering and because it will flower satisfactorily in shady conditions. It grows in the same manner as most of our blackberries, scrambling through the shrubs among which it is planted.

SOLANUM

The most well-known plant of the genus **Solanum** is *S. tuberosum*, which is not known under that name so much as under its vernacular name the Potato. The species that are to be considered here have flowers not dissimilar from the Potato, but in one case they are considerably larger and in the other considerably smaller. Neither are particularly hardy and do better in cold districts with wall protection. Indeed *S. jasminoides* is not suitable for cold districts, although occasional plants may survive where the microclimate is suitable.

Solanum crispum This is a sub-shrub and most of the branches are herbaceous, dying back every winter, except in very mild localities where it behaves as an evergreen. The branches reach a height of 12 ft or more and it bears heads of large mauve potato-like flowers from late June onwards. A selected clone known as 'Glasnevin' (or sometimes as 'autumnalis') is hardier and more floriforous and should be obtained where possible. In most parts of the country the protection of a wall or a paling fence is necessary, and, if this is provided, they will thrive even in cold districts. In milder parts of the country it might be possible to plant it among shrubs, through which it could thrust its long branches. The flowers are followed by yellowish-white berries about the same size as a pea and seed is perhaps the best method of propagation, although cuttings are necessary with selected forms.

The other climbing Solanum, *S. jasminoides* is a twiner and so will appear in chapter 5.

3 Entirely self-supporting

The plants to be considered in this chapter adhere to their host either by means of aerial roots or by means of adhesive disks, which are found at the tips of tendrils. This method of climbing suggests that they ascend the trunks of trees in their native wild state. Of course there is no reason why they should have to do this in the garden and, indeed, these climbers are particularly suitable for growing on walls or for disguising unsightly sheds. They will adhere satisfactorily to brick, stone or cement rendering, although roughcast is not always so satisfactory. However their inherent tendency to climb tree trunks indicates that they are naturally inhabitants of woodland and require shady conditions, particularly around their roots. If they are given walls to climb, they will do well on those facing north or east, but will be less satisfactory on west-facing walls and will only be satisfactory on south walls if these are in the shade of trees.

Although plants such as Ivy do not kill their hosts, as has been suggested, they do seem to inhibit their growth, and the larger plants in this section should only be trained on to well-grown specimens and preferably on those that are not attractive in themselves. They are perhaps even more admirable for clothing dead or dying trees which it is not convenient to remove. Where there are fences of wooden palings, there is a lot to be said for planting ivies at intervals of 8 ft, so that they will hold the fence up and prevent its having to be renewed. Brigadier Lucas Phillips has given this construction the splendid name of a 'fedge'. Although the vast majority of the plants listed in this chapter insist on shady conditions, an exception must be made for the species of Campsis. These will only flower satisfactorily on a south or west facing surface; even so they appreciate shade around the roots and if grown against the house wall may, with advantage, be planted near a corner, so that the roots are against a shady wall, while the branches can be trained on to a sunny surface.

ASTERANTHERA

Asteranthera ovata is a Chilean plant which is by no means easy to grow satisfactorily in this country. It needs a mild climate, an acid soil, a damp atmosphere and nearly perpetual shade. If grown against a wall, it must be a North wall, but it is happier on a tree trunk. It is not a vigorous grower; it is said to reach a height of 15 ft in its native country, but I do not know if such heights have ever been recorded here. It seems equally happy trailing over the ground as climbing a tree or a wall, but apparently is unwilling to flower before it has left the ground. It grows vigorously during the season, but frequently doesn't ripen its wood satisfactorily and much of the growth is liable to be lost during the winter. In the west country, with its mild winter, this is probably of less importance. It is not easy to state how much frost it can tolerate, but it seems to be less intolerant than some writers suggest. Where it does thrive it produces attractive bell-shaped flowers of a carmine-red, about an inch long and 1½ in. across on the old wood. These come at midsummer and continue for some weeks. The plant is evergreen. Any portion of the plant will root in a suitable mixture, so it is easy to detach a piece and keep it through the winter in a cool frost-proof situation. This will prevent the plant being lost, should the winter prove excessively severe. The plant belongs to the Gesneriaceae, which are generally tropical, although there are some European montane genera, such as Ramonda and Haberlea, which are grown on rock gardens. This is a very attractive plant when done well and should certainly be tried by anyone interested in unusual and difficult plants. The leaves are small and produced in some abundance.

CAMPSIS

There are two species of Trumpet Vines, one from North America and the other from China. The two species have been hybridized and the hybrid is perhaps slightly more satisfactory than either of the two species. The plants are perfectly hardy, although young plants should be protected during their first winter (or more advantageously not planted until the spring), but they only flower satisfactorily after a hot dry summer. They are thus best planted on a south or west facing wall. Since the flowers are orange-scarlet in colour, they are not seen at their best against a red brick wall. The plants are deciduous. They flower on the current year's growth and sideshoots should be pruned hard back during the winter. The plant grows quite rapidly but does not flower until it is quite old; it is probably necessary to wait four or five years.

Campsis chinensis This is slightly less hardy than its American brother but has larger and more gorgeous flowers. Indeed it was at one time called *C. grandiflora.* It is the least hardy of the two and, away from very mild districts, needs a south wall. Although it does produce aerial roots, it may well need some extra support, particularly when well established. It is slightly less vigorous than *C. radicans*, seldom exceeding 25 ft, whereas the other species can reach 10 or more ft higher. The flowers are orange-scarlet and appear in August and September.

C. radicans This is the North American counterpart of *C. chinensis* and is hardier and more vigorous, although the flowers are slightly smaller. Various colour forms have been recorded ranging from a bright scarlet (*atropurpurea*) to yellow (*flava*), but the most usual colour is an orange-scarlet. In both species the leaves are pinnate, composed of a number of oval leaflets with toothed edges. At one time there was an early-flowering form of this known, but I am not sure if it is still in cultivation. It should be reintroduced, as it matured its growths earlier and thus proved more reliable in unfavourable summers, when the normal type may not flower at all. The two species have been crossed to give a series of hybrids which have been given the name of **C.×tagliabuana.** The best of these is the cultivar known as 'Madame Galen' which has flowers nearly as large as those of *G. chinensis* and is as hardy as *C. radicans.* The flowers are scarlet with a tinge of salmon and after a hot summer give a splendid display. None of the Campsis are liable to prove satisfactory in cold districts. They may well survive and even grow quite vigorously, but they will not flower. They appear fairly indifferent to the type of soil they are offered.

DECUMARIA

This genus contains only two species, which are related to the climbing hydrangeas. They are somewhat tender and will need the protection of a south or west wall in most districts and they are not really sufficiently decorative to warrant this. Of the species one is North American and one Chinese.

Decumaria barbara This is a fairly vigorous plant, which may reach 30 ft. It is deciduous and has ovate, pointed leaves which may reach a length of 5 in. The small white flowers are produced in corymbs which are about 3 in. across and appear in late June and July.

Decumaria sinensis This is less vigorous, not exceeding 15 ft, and is evergreen in mild districts. The leaves are smaller and more rounded than in the American species and the corymbs may be slightly larger. The flowers have a perfume that is pleasant to some people but repellent to others, so it would be as well to find what your own reaction is, before deciding to invest in a plant.

ERCILLA

This is an evergreen climber that produces a large number of slender stems, that do not branch very much. These stems are thickly covered with rather small leaves, which are ovate, up to 1½ in. long and 1 in. wide. The rather inconspicuous flowers of **E. volubilis** (*Bridgesia spicata*), the only species in cultivation, are produced in spikes which are 1½ in. long. They appear in April, but are followed by purplish berries, which are more attractive. The plant is a native of Chile, but is of much easier cultivation than most Chilean plants. It is excellent for clothing an unsightly shed or out-building and can reach from 15–20 ft. In spite of its aerial roots, it sometimes requires some additional support.

EUONYMUS

Euonymus fortunei var *radicans* is an evergreen climber that has no attractions apart from its leaves. These are not very attractive in the type, being oval and a shining dark green, but there is a silver-variegated form and another variety, *coloratus*, has the leaves turning purple in the autumn. The dwarfer var. *minimus* has leaves only about ¼ in. long and is useful for shady portions of the rock garden. The plant is completely hardy and the type can climb to 20 ft, although the varieties seldom exceed 12 ft. If planted in a light situation they may produce shrubby growths and flowers and fruits. Neither of these latter are very gratifying. The flowers, like those of all Euonymus are inconspicuous, while the fruits are not the brilliant 'spindles' of so many of the more ornamental species. The plant is useful for clothing an unsightly object with evergreen foliage, but otherwise its charm is very restrained.

FICUS

Ficus pumila, popular as a house plant and as a cool greenhouse creeper can be tried out of doors in a few sheltered districts. This like the Euonymus is evergreen and has small ovate dark green leaves, which are close-set along the stems and rather attractive. A shady situation is what this plant needs and it should not be allowed to dry out. It will not stand very much frost and is usually only grown by gardeners in Cornwall and similar sheltered positions. Where conditions allow, it looks attractive on a north wall. The fruiting branches like those of the Euonymus and the Ivies differ in habit and size of leaf from the climbing stems, but they are unlikely to be seen out of doors in this country.

HEDERA

The ivies are all very hardy and can be placed in any position, although it would seem a sad waste to give them a south or a west wall. In spite of some statements, they apparently do no harm to buildings, apart from affording shelter to sparrows and other birds. They may, eventually, damage trees, but even this is not certain. However they certainly spoil the outline of well-grown trees and are best left to those that are for one reason or another unsatisfactory. Since they have no dislike of shade and are very hardy they are particularly useful for clothing north and east walls and the variegated varieties are often very bright in the winter. All the ivies are evergreen. When they have climbed as far as is possible, they produce fruiting branches with rounder leaves and heads of pale green flowers in October and November. The fruiting branches do not produce aerial roots. If a climbing stem is laid along the ground the aerial roots transform themselves into normal roots quite soon, but cuttings, oddly enough, often take a surprisingly long time to root.

Hedera canariensis One would imagine that an Ivy from the Canary Islands would prove tender in this country and it is so described in many gardening books, but without any justification. A plant of the variegated form in my garden was unmoved by the winter of 1962–3 and since I live in a cold district I imagine it can be regarded as hardy anywhere. The silver variegated form is often grown as a house plant and there is another cultivar with the name 'Golden Leaf'; but the name does not describe the colour, which is bright green with a lighter patch in the centre of the leaf, which it would be flattering to call golden. The normal green-leaved type used to appear as *H. helix* 'Ravenholst', but is not now much grown. The leaves of all the different forms are large and roughly triangular in shape, although they may be slightly lobed.

No variegated ivy makes its best appearance in very heavy shade; some light seems to be necessary for the variegation to be really marked. The green-leaved ivies will grow happily in the deepest shade and so, for that matter, will the variegated types, but these latter look more conspicuous when given a certain amount of light. They are still satisfactory for north walls, provided these are not themselves shaded.

Hedera colchica This is by far the largest-leaved ivy in cultivation and so needs a large expanse to make its full effect. The leaves are practically unlobed and reach a length of 8 in. and a width of 6 in. There are two cultivars; one with variegated leaves and the other with the edges of the leaves slightly toothed.

Hedera helix This is the common Ivy of our woods and hedges, which is known in a very large number of cultivated forms. They may, however be briefly classified into three categories: those with silver variegation, those with yellow variegation, and those with green leaves of uncharacteristic shape. The last category is the least numerous, but includes the arrow-head shaped *sagittaefolia*, the nearly unlobed *deltoides* and the crested *cristata*. The variegated forms can be distinguished into those forms in which the variegation is chiefly around the edge of the leaves and those which have the whole surface suffused. These latter are generally termed *marmorata*, which suggests that their namers thought that the leaves were veined like marble. There is some confusion about the various cultivar names and it is best to visit a nursery or garden centre and select the plants you require.

Hedera hibernica The Irish Ivy is not easy to distinguish from *H. helix*, but in general the leaves are larger; the average width of the English Ivy is around 4 in. while the Irish Ivy is 2 in. wider. There seems to be only one variegated form (*maculata*) recorded. As has already been mentioned, once the ivy has climbed to the summit of its host, it starts to produce fruiting branches. These are characterised by unlobed leaves and the stems do not bear aerial roots. If cuttings are taken of these fruiting branches, these same characteristics persist and you can grow what used to be described as 'tree ivies'. These are not trees, so much as shrubs, but they do make self-contained plants needing no support. The flowers of the Ivy are greenish and they are generally followed by black berries. There is, however, an exception in **Hedera nepalensis**, the Himalayan Ivy. This does not differ notably in appearance from other ivies, although the leaves are never deeply lobed. Its main attraction lies in the berries, which are either yellow or red in colour. It is therefore best planted against a fairly low support in a well-lit position, so that it can be hurried into its fruiting state.

For the majority of ivies, the attraction lies in the variegated leaves and they should be inspected from time to time, and any unvariegated growths should be cut out at once. The cultivar known as 'Golden Jubilee' does not show its deep yellow variegation until the leaf is well-developed and this must be borne in mind, otherwise you may cut out perfectly good growths.

HYDRANGEA

There are three species of climbing Hydrangea known, two of which are very similar in appearance, while the third is not particularly attractive and may be no longer in commerce.

Hydrangea anomala This plant, a native of the Himalayas and China, is not very different from the better-known *H. petiolaris*, but it is slightly less vigorous and has fewer stamens. It is a deciduous climber that may reach 40 ft or more in height, but which, if trained over a tree stump, will flower at a reasonable height. All these climbing hydrangeas are sometimes rather slow in starting to grow, but once they have started they proceed quite rapidly. The corymbs of flowers are white and are produced on lateral growths. They consist of a number of small fertile flowers surrounded by much larger sterile flowers, like the 'Lace-cap' Hydrangeas. The plant is less satisfactory than its better-known Japanese brother. It is suitable for similar situations.

Hydrangea integerrima This Chilean plant is possibly no longer in commerce. Unlike the two Asiatic species it is evergreen, with leathery leaves that can reach a length of 6 in. and which are oval in shape. Unfortunately the flowers are not very attractive. The fertile flowers are greenish in colour and there are only occasional white sterile flowers, so that the plant is not very conspicuous in flower.

Hydrangea petiolaris This Japanese plant can reach great heights if necessary. There have apparently been records of its reaching 80 ft. It may be trained up trees or on a north or east wall. If given an old tree stump, it does not get so high and comes into flower more rapidly. The white flowers are like those of *H. anomala*, but slightly larger, and the sterile flowers are quite noticeably larger. An attraction of both the Asiatic species is the peeling bark, which gives interest to the trunk. All the climbing hydrangeas flower in June and none can be recommended for people who want quick results. Even under the most favourable conditions, it will almost certainly be at least five years before any flowers can be expected. On the other hand a well-grown specimen of this is most imposing, although I, personally, would prefer the rather similar *Schizophragma hydrangeoides*, to which we will come shortly.

PARTHENOCISSUS

This genus contains plants formerly known as *Ampelopsis* or *Vitis* and most of them have adhesive tips to the tendrils, so that they can adhere to a tree or a wall without any other support. Most of the vine family climb by means of tendrils and will be found in the next chapter. Although after a hot summer they may bear small bunches of bluish small grapes, they are grown entirely for the beauty of their leaves, either throughout the season as in *P. henryana* or in the autumn as in the popular *P. tricuspidata*. With one exception they are perfectly hardy.

Parthenocissus henryana. Although this species lacks the brilliant autumn colour of most of the others, it is in many ways more attractive, as the leaves are delightfully variegated with silver-white along the principal veins. It is, however, necessary to have the plant in a shady position, as otherwise the variegation is liable to be suppressed. It is thus an ideal plant for a north or an east wall. The leaves are composed of from 3–5 leaflets, which are not very large in young plants, but which may attain a length of 5 in. in mature specimens. The leaves are an attractive purplish colour when they emerge and then they become dark green, against which the silver veins shine out. All parthenocissus are vigorous climbers, but *P. henryana* is more restrained than some of the others.

P. himalayana This is the only tender species and it needs the protection of a wall. It has a leaf composed of 3 leaflets, which are dark green. In the variety *rubrifolia*, the young leaves are purplish while they are developing and this is the best variety to grow. The autumn colour is a very brilliant scarlet.

Parthenocissus quinquefolia All the Parthenocissus are known familiarly as Virginian Creepers, but this is the species that actually comes from Virginia. The others are Asiatic. (There is another American species, but this, *P. vitacea*, does not have adhesive disks). The true Virginian Creeper is a very vigorous climber with, as its specific name suggests, leaves composed of 5 leaflets. This is a splendid sight in the autumn when the leaves turn scarlet and looks well among large trees. It is rather too vigorous for a house wall.

P. thomsonii This is the least vigorous of all the self supporting species, yet is still quite vivacious. It is also one of the most ornamental, as the young leaves and young shoots are a reddish purple. The leaves become a rather dull purple as they mature and then take on reddish hues in the autumn. Unless a very vigorous climber is needed, this is the best for use around the house, although *P. henryana* might well be preferred for a shady wall. The leaves are similar in shape and size to the other species, being composed of 5 oval leaflets, each about 4 in. long.

P. tricuspidata. This is, perhaps, the most popular of the Virginian Creepers. The leaves are of different shapes, some are entire, while others consist of three leaflets. The lower leaves are often very wide, sometimes 10 in. across, while the normal leaves are about half this width. The variety *lowii* has much smaller leaves, which are lobed and resemble those of a vine. Both the type and its variety are very brilliant in the autumn.

All the Parthenocissus are very easily grown and seem indifferent to the type of soil in which they are planted. If one has a tall Yew hedge, they show up to great advantage if allowed to ramble through this and make it look very brilliant in the autumn. Some people tend to despise them because they are so easily grown, but it seems an illogical attitude to take up. It seems to be a form of garden snobbery to look down on plants, however attractive they may be, if they are easy to grow. This attitude seems very ungrateful to me. If a plant is attractive and easy to grow it has two virtues. The attraction of Parthenocissus lies entirely in the leaf shape and the brilliant autumn colours, but that does not make the genus despicable.

PILEOSTEGIA

There is only one species in cultivation and this is **Pileostegia viburnoides.** The genus is related to Hydrangea and Schizophragma, but the inflorescence lacks any showy sterile flowers and the plant is evergreen. It is also considerably less vigorous, seldom growing more than 10 ft high, although a height of 20 ft has been recorded. The small flowers are white and come in large panicles, so that the plant is quite showy, although the individual flowers are so small. The dark green leaves are leathery, a long oval in shape, and may reach a length of 6 in. The plant is perfectly hardy but needs a rather rich soil and will not thrive in shallow chalky soils. It probably prefers soil that is slightly acid, but grows adequately where the reaction is alkaline. The plant is particularly valuable on account of its late flowering; it comes into flower in late August and in September, at a time when there are few flowering shrubs of any description in flower. Owing to its modest dimensions, it is a very suitable climber for bungalows. It is by no means a rapid grower, but starts flowering at an early age. It is easily propagated by cuttings.

SCHIZOPHRAGMA

The plants in this genus are very similar in growth and in appearance to the climbing hydrangeas, from which they differ in the sterile flowers being composed of a single bract in Schizophragma, while those of Hydrangea consist of four bracts.

Schizophragma hydrangeoides This can reach a height of 40 ft and the deciduous leaves are broadly ovate and have a toothed edge. The flowers are yellowish white and are in heads up to 8 in. across, with the sterile flowers up to 1½ in. long. Like the other species in cultivation, it is deciduous and flowers in July, a month later than the climbing hydrangeas.

Schizophragma integrifolia Although this is slightly less vigorous than the last species—it seldom exceeds 30 ft—this has a far more conspicuous inflorescence and is in every way a more desirable plant. The flowering heads may be as much as a foot across and the sterile bracts are 3 in. long and so make a very brave display. The colour is a pure white without the yellow tinge of *S. hydrangeoides*. The leaves are only very finely toothed or, sometimes, not at all and so the plant can be distinguished from the former species when it is not in flower. The leaves of *S. hydrangeoides* are coarsely toothed. This is a really first class climber and should be tried wherever sufficient space is available.

Both species like a rich cool root-run, but are perfectly hardy even in the coldest districts. They start to flower at an earlier age than the climbing hydrangeas and, in my opinion, are decidedly preferable.

1 *Abutilon megapotamicum*

2 *Codonopsis tangshen*

3 *Hedera helix* 'Silver Queen'

4 *Hedera helix* 'Buttercup'

5 Pillar Rose 'Elegance'

6 *Rosa helenae*

7 *Clematis macropetala*

8 *Campsis* 'Mme Galen' rioting over a gateway

9 *Clematis tangutica*

10 *Clematis* 'Lasurstern': a *patens* hybrid

11 Rose 'Mermaid'

12 *Actinidia chinensis*

13 *Pileostegia viburnoides*

14 *Hydrangea integerrima*

15 *Wisteria floribunda alba*

16 *Lonicera tragophyll*

4 Hand over hand

The climbers to be considered in this chapter are those which ascend by means of tendrils, which cling on to their host. These may be specially adapted leaves, forming true tendrils, or they may attach themselves by means of twisting the leaf stalk. This method of climbing requires a profusion of rather thin twiggy growths on which the tendrils can fasten. They are evidently not adapted for growing directly up trees, although they may progress happily once they have got among the young wood of trees, but it must be clear that no tendril or petiole could ever encircle a tree trunk. We may assume therefore that in the wild they are to be found most frequently among scrub and low shrubs. If, however, there are young trees among the scrub it may well be that these plants will ascend with the trees, so that we get a climber that is attached to its host only at the top, the lower portion having become almost trunk-like. Some of the tendrilled climbers such as many Vitis species and *Clematis montana* are very vigorous and require a lot of space to display themselves and we may well wish to train them into trees. In this case they must be trained up some supports to start with, such as a long cane. They will have to be tied to this, as the tendrils will not be sufficient to hold the plant upright at this stage. It is, of course possible to put something like pea boughs or brushwood to support the plant in the early stages, but it will probably be desirable to remove this support later, when the plant has established itself among the branches and it is simpler to undo the ties and remove the cane than to try and disentangle the plant from pea boughs.

The less vigorous clingers can be trained in shrubs or in hedges and will probably need little support, although even here a cane may be necessary for the first year or so. In windy districts there is always a risk of clematis snapping off in a gale and it is advisable to leave the support for a few years, until the basal trunk is sufficiently thick and tough to resist any gale. They are surprisingly resilient and it is only in the young plant that wind damage is liable to be a danger. However the *Atragene* section (*Cc. alpina* and *macropetala*) never make very thick trunks and, if there is a risk of wind damage, they will need almost a permanent support at the base. This is not necessary if they are growing on walls, but is advisable if they are clambering into shrubs. In the wild it is quite unusual to see *Clematis alpina* growing erect; it is more liable to ramble through some low shrub, such as the Alpine Rose or a Juniper. Under these circumstances the lower parts of the stems are protected by the host from fierce winds and there is much to be said for imitating this method of growth in the garden. You will find *C. alpina* climbing in forests, where the wind force will be reduced by all the trees, but in exposed positions it attaches itself to dwarf, spreading shrubs.

The plants in the two previous chapters have all been shrubby, but there are a few herbaceous climbers that ascend by means of tendrils; some annual and some perennial. It is probably more convenient to put these in a separate section and so this chapter will have two sections, one devoted to the shrubby climbers and one to the herbaceous.

I SHRUBBY TENDRILLED CLIMBERS

This section includes the numerous members of the Vine family, although few gardeners will wish to have all the available species, there are a large number from which to choose. Also in this section are the Clematis, of which it might be argued that it is difficult to have too many.

AMPELOPSIS

Ampelopsis is distinguished from the true vines, *Vitis* spp, by the structure of their flowers. They are all deciduous climbers which will grow in any deep soil. Some plants are very vigorous, while others are comparatively restrained.

Ampelopsis aconitifolia This is one of the less vigorous species, although it can cover a 20 ft wall in time. It is grown principally on account of its elegant fern-like foliage. Each leaf is composed of from 3 to 5 leaflets, which may be 3 in. long. Each leaflet is very deeply lobed and the edges of the leaflets are toothed, so the general impression is light and airy. After a hot summer the plant produces a further attraction in its bunches of small yellow or orange 'grapes'. These are individually only about ¼ in. long, but since they appear in small bunches they are quite conspicuous.

Ampelopsis bodinieri (micans) This will barely reach 20 ft in height and has handsome purplish young growth. The dark, shining leaves are only slightly 3-lobed and are borne on purple petioles. They may reach a length of 5 in. This is not one of the most attractive species, but the shining leaves have a rather quiet charm.

Ampelopsis brevipedunculata (heterophylla) The form most commonly grown is var. *maximowiczii*, but is more generally met with under the name of *A. heterophylla.* This is a very vigorous climber, with reddish young growth and leaves of very varying shapes, which gives the plant its main fascination. The same plant may carry unlobed leaves, leaves which are only slightly lobed and leaves that are very deeply lobed. The individual leaves are not very large. There are two other varieties which are sometimes seen. Var. *citrulloides* has the leaves very deeply lobed and these lobes may be lobed themselves, so that the plant has a rather ferny effect. Var. *elegans* is a much weaker plant with the leaves variegated with pink and white; the colour of these leaves is very attractive, but they always look slightly distorted and unhealthy. After a hot summer the type may bear numerous bunches of brilliant blue grapes, which look very attractive.

Ampelopsis chaffanjonii (watsoniana) Although the leaves are not so enormous as in the next species, they are often a foot in length and are composed of up to 7 leaflets arranged pinnately. This is a plant that is best grown into a tree as the leaves have a purple underside. The plant has brilliant autumn colours. As might be expected of a plant with such large leaves, it is fairly vigorous.

Ampelopsis megalophylla This is the most vigorous species and is capable of reaching a height of 40 ft. The pinnate leaves may reach a length of 2 ft and are composed of numerous ovate leaflets that may be 6 in. long and half as wide. It is grown entirely on account of its magnificent leaves, but needs plenty of room in which to display them. This is a magnificent shrub, but not one which it is easy to place in a small garden.

Ampelopsis orientalis This is a rather weak climber from Asia Minor, again with pinnate leaves, but they are not so large as in the two previous species. They are however fairly sizeable and can on occasion reach a foot in length. The fruits resemble red currants and are attractive when produced. *A. orientalis* is the least vigorous of the pinnate leaved species, and is at its best scrambling through medium-sized shrubs.

BIGNONIA

Botanists seem unable to decide whether the plant usually known as **Bignonia capreolata** should be allowed to retain its name or be called *Doxantha.* In any case it is a fairly vigorous climber, which is evergreen in mild localities, but deciduous in colder climes. In most parts of the British Isles it needs a south-facing wall and, like Campsis, will only flower well following a hot summer. The orange, trumpet shaped flowers (purple in the var. *atrosanguinea*) appear from the leaf axils in June. Although it is said to reach 40 ft in the S.E. United States, where it is native, it rarely exceeds 25 ft here, even in favoured localities. In the United States it is known as the Cross Vine, as a cross can be seen in the wood if the trunk is cut.

CLEMATIS

This is arguably the most popular genus of climbing plants to be found in gardens. Apart from the dreaded wilt disease they are trouble free, and all but a few species are hardy anywhere in the British Isles. Most of the species will grow well on the chalk and they all seem indifferent to the presence of lime in the soil. Since most of the European species are definitely lime lovers it was assumed at one time that lime was necessary for all Clematis, but this is not correct. Even in Europe *C. alpina* can be found growing happily in acid soil and some of the Asiatic species are also to be found in such soils in their native haunts. All of the climbing species have their roots in the shade, out of which they climb to produce their flowers and similar situations should be provided in the garden if it is possible. If you want to grow Clematis against a hot wall, put a paving slab over the roots in an attempt to keep the root run cool and moist. There is always a risk of mildew disfiguring the plants if Clematis are grown against a wall and they will show themselves off to more advantage in other situations. However this is not always possible and if they are to be grown against the house they will need either another plant to grow up or a wire mesh support. The large-flowered hybrid Clematis are based on two Chinese species which are not themselves in cultivation any longer. The early flowering hybrids were based on *C. patens* and the later flowering ones on *C. lanuginosa.*

If Clematis are trained through shrubs or into trees they will not need pruning, but it will probably be necessary to prune when they are grown against walls. A simple rule of pruning is to prune all Clematis that flower before the end of June as soon as flowering is finished, while the later flowering kinds are pruned in the winter. The late flowering types are usually pruned very hard, while the early flowering ones are treated more lightly, although they too can be pruned quite hard if necessary. The late flowering sorts produce their flowers at the end of the current year's growth and hard pruning of established plants will encourage the formation of plenty of new wood on which the flowers will appear. The early-flowering sorts produce their flowers on laterals from year-old wood and so it is not always advisable to prune these so hard, as should the summer prove cold and wet, the new wood may not always be sufficiently ripened. Since this class will often produce strong shoots without any pruning, it is possible to leave the pruning of the early summer flowering hybrids until the winter. This then entails removing most of any two-year-old growths and leaving all the one-year-old shoots.

The late flowering species and hybrids are usually cut down to within about three feet of the ground.

Clematis wilt is the great danger in growing the large flowered hybrids; the species appear to be immune. It is apparently due to a fungus infection, which girdles the main stem and prevents any nourishment from either going up or coming down. The fungus starts in dead tissues, so it is a routine precaution to cut out all dead wood that may be visible. It is also recommended to put the plants in the soil rather lower than when they are received from the nursery. This means that there are some dormant buds available under the soil, should the wilt kill all the aerial portion of the plant and these will break through the soil and give one a second chance. Wilt attacks the plants most frequently in the first year, but two or three-year-old plants are not immune, although once one has had the plant in the garden for three years, one can usually relax.

Clematis are always sold growing in containers, so that they can be put in the garden at any time. However there is much to be said in favour of planting them in the autumn. After planting they are usually cut down to about 9–12 in. This should also be done if they are planted in the spring, but it may already have been done in the nursery, before the plant is sent out. During their first year it is necessary to see that the young plants do not dry out, as they are intolerant of drought and you may lose your plant if it is too prolonged. North walls are very suitable for most Clematis, although the yellow-flowered species such as *tangutica* and *orientalis* will not flower very freely in the shade. The large-flowered hybrids will all do excellently on a north wall, particularly the earlier flowering *patens* hybrids.

Clematis climb by twisting the leaf stalks round the twigs of their host, so if they are trained to a wall or other structure they must be given something on which to cling. Plastic-covered wire netting has the advantage of not looking unattractive before it is covered. Galvanized sheep netting is somewhat cheaper, but a slight eyesore. These are usually fitted to wooden battens or to vine eyes, so that they are not flush with the wall.

By no means all the species are in cultivation and the list that follows is confined to those that may be obtainable either as plants or as seeds.

Clematis afoliata (aphylla) A strange species from New Zealand, which needs the protection of a south or west wall and which is very hard to obtain. It grows only to about 6 ft and has either no leaves at all or extremely small ones. From the axils it produces heads of about 6 greenish-white fragrant flowers, which are an inch across. The plant is a curiosity rather than anything else.

Clematis alpina A scrambler rather than a climber, which is happiest if given some low spreading shrub over which it can grow. This is a very delightful plant growing up to 8 ft with nodding powder blue flowers in late April; it is among the first Clematis to appear. It belongs to the section *Atragene* which have not only coloured tepals (petal-like sepals) as do all the other Clematis, but also a number of petal-like stamens (petaloid staminodes) which give the flowers a semi-double appearance. *C. macropetala* is very similar. A white form is known, which is sometimes given the name var. *sibirica*, but it is not a very good white and the blue forms are preferable.

Clematis armandii This is one of the few Clematis that are evergreen. It is a vigorous climber, capable of reaching 30 ft, and is regarded as being somewhat tender. However this tenderness does not seem to be consistent and one sometimes sees splendid plants growing in the most unlikely places. It is very temperamental and, according to that great gardener, the late Sir Frederick Stern, it must be allowed to grow as it wishes. Any attempt to train it to your wishes is liable to cause a fit of temper and the plant dies. A site should therefore be provided for it which gives it plenty of room and a certain amount of shelter. As it may decide to grow untidily, it should be given a situation where there is ample room and where an untidy mat of clambering stems will not be out of place.

The evergreen leaves are composed of three leaflets, which are oblong oval in shape and up to 5 in. long. They are a dark glossy green, except in the cultivar 'Apple Blossom', when they are bronzy. The flowers are white in the type, pale pink in 'Apple Blossom', about 2 in. across and produced in dense clusters from the leaf axils. This is an early flowerer and is usually at its best at the end of April. Once planted it should be left severely alone.

Clematis balearica (calycina) Although botanists now regard this as a subspecies of *C. cirrhosa*, it is usually listed as a separate species. This is an evergreen climber found wild in Minorca and Corsica. It is attractive on account of its small fern-like leaves and for the fact that it flowers during the winter months, between November and March. The flowers themselves are not very showy. They are about 2 in. across and a greeny-yellow in colour, with purple spots on the inside. They are never produced in any great profusion, but since they come at a time when any flowers are welcome, they are not to be despised. The fern like leaves are basically ternate or biternate, but the individual leaflets are deeply lobed and the plant is attractive for its foliage apart from its winter flowers. It is only moderately vigorous, usually reaching about 10 ft in height. It is considerably hardier than its habitats would suggest. Plants went happily through the 1962–3 winter. However though it will grow in most districts, it only flowers freely in mild parts unless given the protection of a wall.

Clematis buchananiana This seems rather a mysterious species. Seeds are listed by one of our most well-known seedsmen but the plant is not described in the R.H.S.Dictionary of Gardening. It is however, referred to in Bailey's Hortus Second. It sounds as though it were similar to *C. montana*. It is described as vigorous and deciduous, with hairy leaves, which are pinnate with toothed or lobed leaflets and white flowers about 2½ in. across in panicles. Neither the seedsman nor Bailey gives the time of flowering, but one would expect it to be at the same time as *montana* and *chrysocoma* about mid-May.

Clematis campaniflora. This is a Portuguese plant, related to *C. viticella*, but with very small nodding flowers that are of so pale a lavender hue, that they appear to be nearly white. The plant is deciduous and very vigorous and should be given a rather large shrub through which it can scramble. It is not sufficiently showy to be given a very prominent place. Although it produces a large number of flowers it does this over a long period and there is never an eye-taking display. It is valuable however for the fact that these flowers are produced from August until October and so it is flowering at a time when few other Clematis are out. This plant responds well to quite severe pruning in February, otherwise it is liable to become rather leggy. It can reach a height of 20 ft if that is desired. The plant is perfectly hardy, but some of the current year's wood might be killed in a severe winter. It flowers on the year's current growth, so no damage is done if some of this is cut back during the winter.

Clematis chrysocoma This is a dwarf version of *C. montana.* It seldom exceeds 8 ft in height and has the young stems and the immature leaves, the leaf and flower stalks all covered with a dense brownish-yellow down. The flowers are white with a pink flush and are produced from July onwards. It is somewhat tender and in cold districts it is best replaced by its hybrid with *C. montana*, known as *C.* × *vedrariensis.* This is quite vigorous and is May flowering, so that it is not altogether satisfactory as a replacement. Its modest dimensions make *C. chrysocoma* very suitable for growing against a wall. *Clematis spooneri* is sometimes called *C. chrysocoma* var. *sericea*, but since it is very vigorous and flowers in May, it would seem more reasonable to continue to give it specific rank.

Clematis cirrhosa This is an evergreen scrambler found around the Mediterranean, where it is usually scrambling among low shrubs such as Cistus and Rosemary. The creamy-green flowers are produced in March or even earlier in mild winters. They are about 2 in. across and are not displayed very conspicuously. Although the plant is frost hardy, it only flowers satisfactorily after a hot summer and is not a very satisfactory garden plant, in spite of its early flowering. The leaves are far less attractive than those of *C. balearica* and this latter is also more floriferous and therefore preferable.

Clematis fargesii An attractive climber of the *montana* group with very large leaves and a succession of flowers from June to September. The leaves are composed of 9 leaflets and may be 9 in.

long while the individual leaflets are up to 2½ in. long. The young shoots are purplish in colour. The white flowers are up to 2½ in. across and are borne either singly or in few-flowered clusters from the leaf axils. It is capable of climbing to a height of 20 ft, so it is quite a vigorous plant. It is very attractive and is especially valuable for its long flowering season.

Clematis flammula Although a Mediterranean plant, this has proved perfectly hardy and has even naturalized itself in some parts. It is deciduous in this country, although semi-evergreen in the wild and will grow to 10 feet. It tends to make a leggy plant, if not pruned regularly, and is at its best scrambling through low shrubs. The individual flowers are small, but they are produced in large heads and are very fragrant. They are a shining white in colour. It is chiefly on account of its fragrance that the plant is grown. It has been hybridized with *C. viticella* to give the plant known either as *C.×rubro-marginata* or as *C.×violacea rubro-marginata*. This has the same fragrance, but has larger flowers that are violet with a white base. It is thus a far more attractive plant. Both the species and the hybrid are autumn-flowerers.

Clematis florida This is the only one of the parents of the large-flowered hybrids that is still in cultivation, although it is thought to differ somewhat from the wild form. The plants in cultivation were introduced from Japanese gardens. The species itself is a native of China. The cultivated plant is sometimes semi-evergreen, but more usually deciduous, with leaves 5 in. long composed of 9 leaflets. The flowers are about 3 in. across and are white with a greenish band down the centre of the back of the tepals. The plant most often seen is the var. *sieboldii* (*bicolor*) which has the centre filled with purple petaloid staminodes. Although the plant has a reputation for being tender, this is apparently unjustified. It will tolerate plenty of frost. It does, however, require a rich soil and will not thrive in hot sandy or chalky soils. The flowers usually appear in July, although some forms flower in June.

Clematis indivisa This is another of the New Zealand Clematis and can only be grown successfully in Southern England, westward from Sussex. The plant is a vigorous evergreen climber and, unlike the majority of the genus, is dioecious. The plants with the male flowers are the more conspicuous. The leaf is composed of 3 leaflets, which are entire in the type, but lobed in the var. *lobata*, which is larger and hardier. The white flowers may be 3 in. across and are produced in axillary panicles in May and June. The plant is thus extremely desirable and should be grown, where it is possible. It seems to be happier among tall shrubs than it is against a wall and should not be pruned or interfered with.

Clematis koreana Although easily grown from seed, this is not a very decorative plant. It is rather a weak climber and does not reach more than 10 ft. The flowers are produced singly and are not large. The colour of the flowers is variable, some being purplish while others are a greenish-yellow. The plant belongs to the *Atragene* section and has a semi-double appearance. The flowers appear in August and September.

Clematis lanuginosa This is the main parent of the large-flowered, late-flowering hybrids. The popular *C.×jackmannii* for example is *lanuginosa* pollinated by *viticella*. The species itself is no longer in cultivation, but its presence in hybrids can usually be recognized by the large oval leaflets, which are heart-shaped at the base. Wild forms vary in colour from white to quite a deep mauve and some forms flower as early as June, while others were said to flower as late as October.

Clematis macropetala This is a Chinese plant allied to *C. alpina*, which it resembles in many ways, but is larger and more vigorous. The nodding flowers are produced in late April and May and are powder-blue in colour with rather paler staminodes. There are selected forms of different colours such as the deep blue 'Maidwell Hall' and the pinkish 'Markhamii'. The plant will climb to about 12 ft and the individual flowers are from 3–4 in. across. The plant is perfectly hardy and never fails to give a good display. Occasionally there are a few flowers produced in the autumn. This is probably the most delightful of the spring flowering species and should be a first choice with anyone. It seems to display itself best when planted against a wall or a fence.

Clematis montana This is probably the most vigorous of all Clematis; if trained into a tree it will easily reach a height of 40 ft and is a very rapid grower. It is deciduous and the leaves are composed of 3 leaflets. The flowers are produced in large clusters from the leaf axils and are each about 2 in. across. They are pure white in the type, but there are coloured forms known such as the lilac *lilacina*, the pink *rubens*, which has the additional advantage of purplish leaves and the large-flowered pinky-mauve 'Tetrarose'. There is also a curious variety, *wilsonii*, with white flowers, 3 in. across, which are not produced until July or August. Most forms come into flower in May or early June. This is a plant requiring a certain amount of space . . . it can, of course be controlled by pruning . . . but if this can be given there are few plants that are more reliable or more decorative.

Clematis orientalis This plant is found in the wild from the Caucasus to China and is, not unnaturally, very variable. Some forms are delightful, while others are less attractive. It is a vigorous climber, capable of reaching 20 ft and has fern-like leaves that may be 8 in. long and which are composed of small leaflets, set rather far apart. The flowers are yellow, rather nodding and about 2 in. across. Some forms have purple stamens which add to the attraction. The most popular form is that sent back by Ludlow and Sheriff under the number 13342. This has the tepals nearly ¼ in. thick, which explains its popular name of the 'Lemon-peel Clematis'. The colour, however, is rather a pale lemon and there are other forms in cultivation with thinner tepals of a better yellow colour. The plant starts to flower in late July and continues until October. This, like the other yellow-flowered species (*tangutica* and *serratifolia*) will only produce their flowers when they have emerged into the light and should be given a rather sunnier position than is necessary for most of the other species.

Clematis paniculata This Japanese species is obtainable, although it is seldom satisfactory in this country. It is a very vigorous grower, capable of reaching 30 ft or more and produces axillary panicles of small white flowers in September and October. In districts with a hot summer this is apparently a very splendid sight, but in this country it seldom seems to flower with much freedom, although it is easy enough to grow. In many ways it is like a very vigorous *C. flammula* and the flowers have a perfume like that of hawthorn.

Clematis patens This Japanese species is the main parent of the early-flowering large-flowered hybrids, but the species itself is not in cultivation. The typical wild form is said to have white flowers, but most of the forms that were introduced were either pale or deep violet. The species had flowers up to 6 in. across and appeared in May and June.

Clematis rehderiana This plant is remarkably photogenic and many people must have been induced to purchase it from seeing a photograph. It is a vigorous deciduous climber, capable of reaching 30 ft, with pinnate leaves that may be 9 in. long and are composed of from 7 to 9 leaflets. The flowers are produced in erect panicles arising from the leaf axils and are rather small and bell-like in shape. They are a greenish-yellow, sometimes described as primrose-yellow and are said to have a perfume of cowslips. We all have blind areas in our noses and I have never been able to perceive this scent. The plant starts to flower in late July and continues until September. In flower it looks very different from most Clematis, but it is not very showy and it would not be an obvious choice for the small garden. Where one has plenty of space it is a different matter, particularly if you can smell the flowers.

Clematis serratifolia This is scarcely distinct from *C. tangutica* and comes from Korea. It is fairly vigorous and has rather small yellow flowers in August and September. It is thus later than *C. tangutica* and the flowers are a brighter yellow than those of *C. orientalis*, so the plant has a definite value. It is not, however, so good a plant as *C. tangutica* and where there is only room for one, there should be no hesitation.

Clematis spooneri This is a vigorous, but fairly slow-growing, climber related to *C. montana.* The young shoots and the stems are covered with down like those of *C. chrysocoma*, but this tends to be silvery and is not nearly so thick. The leaves are rather larger than those of *C. montana* and appear to be more hairy. The flowers are larger, up to 3 in. across and show the same variation in colour, although the white forms are typical. Even when full-grown the plant will not exceed 20 ft in height and so it is the best substitute for *C. montana* where space is limited. It flowers in May, usually about a week later than *C. montana.*

Clematis tangutica A vigorous deciduous climber that can reach from 15 to 20 ft quite rapidly. It is one of the most attractive of clematis not only for its nodding yellow flowers but also for the grey feathery seed-heads which succeed the flowers. In this way the plant has two seasons when it looks attractive. The flowers are at their best in late June and early July and the seed heads continue to look attractive until September. This is an admirable plant in many ways it starts to flower when it is small and is no trouble. It is probably most people's first choice after the large flowered hybrids and, since there are no large-flowered yellow Clematis, it brings a new colour into the range available.

Clematis texensis The species is not in cultivation at the present time, though it is to be hoped that it will soon be re-introduced. In Texas it is quite a vigorous climber, but in this country it tended to die down to the roots every year and this character has been transmitted to many of its hybrids, which are in cultivation and which will be mentioned shortly. The plant belongs to the section *Viorna*, which appears to be confined to the U.S.A. In this section the flowers are urn-shaped and nodding and do not open to any large extent. This latter character is found in many of the smaller flowered hybrids. The great attraction of this species is the unusual colour, it is somewhat variable, but in its best forms the colour is scarlet. In all the forms it is some shade of red. When it was in cultivation it proved to be tender and needed the protection of a south or west wall. In an attempt to breed this colour in to the large flowered hybrids, it was crossed both with *patens* and *lanuginosa* and with various hybrids giving rise to such plants as 'Ville de Lyon' with claret coloured flowers. There are also hybrids with smaller-flowered species—though which do not seem to be recorded—and this has given rise to plants with colours of a better shade of red. The best is 'Etoile Rose', with cerise flowers that open fairly widely and the slightly larger-flowered 'Gravetye Beauty'. These die down each year and so seldom exceed 8 ft in height and do better with wall protection. In any case as much sun as can be provided is necessary to induce flower buds to form. 'Countess of Onslow' and 'Duchess of Albany' tend to be more woody, but the long pink flowers never open properly and they are less attractive. They are very liable to get mildew badly when grown on walls and might do better if trained against a fence facing in the right direction.

Clematis viorna It is rather curious that this, not very attractive, species should be in cultivation, while the more attractive *C. pitcheri* is not. It is this species which gave the name to the *Viorna* group of Clematis. The plant climbs from 6 to 10 ft but the stems die back each winter to the woody base of the plant. The nodding urn-shaped flowers are about 1¼in. long and composed of thick tepals, which are reddish-purple in colour. They are produced continuously from May until August, but never have many flowers out at any one time.

Clematis viticella This can be a very vigorous climber if planted in a shady situation, but is more controlled if placed in a well-lit position. In this latter position it will not exceed 12 ft, whereas otherwise it can get considerably higher. The rather small, nodding flowers are about 1½in. across and, in the type, are a rich violet in colour. However there are several reddish variants known under the varietal names *rubra* and *kermesina*. There are also some hybrids with slightly larger flowers, of which the nearly white 'alba luxurians' is the best, in my opinion. Although the individual flowers are small, they are produced in great abundance and the plant looks extremely attractive in late July and August. The plant definitely gains from rather hard pruning in February. Much of the new wood will die back during the winter in any case, so it is easier to prune the plant back, than to go round cutting out the dead wood later. The seeds of this Clematis differ from those of most other species, by being rather large and flat and in lacking the feathery covering that the others have. These germinate well and seed is one of the easiest means of increasing this Clematis. Although we have not exhausted the list of existing species, it is not very likely that many of the others will be available. A few tender species such as *C. colensoi*, *C. pavoliniana* and *C. uncinata* are sometimes available, but are not likely to be of much interest, except to those who wish to specialize in the genus. *C. pavoliniana* is the most attractive, being similar to *C. armandii*, but flowering in June. At one time *C. columbiana*, an American species close to *C. alpina*, was in commerce, but I have not seen it listed for some time.

Clematis are fairly easily propagated by cuttings of half-ripened growths. It seems a matter of luck whether these root easier if trimmed off at a node or between the nodes; some have more success in one way and some in the other. The difficulty comes when the rooted cutting is transferred, either to a pot or to its final position in the garden. The roots are brittle and the plants resent root disturbance, so care is needed during this operation, and, if the cutting is to be placed in its final home, it should be given a light soil mixture immediately round the root ball so as to encourage rapid root growth and get the plant to establish itself.

MUTISIA

This is a genus of climbers belonging to the Daisy family, the Compositae, a very large family among which there are very few climbers. They are all natives of S. America and have a reputation for tenderness, which does not seem altogether deserved. Plants against a south wall thrive as far north as Inverness and Brigadier Lucas Phillips records that a plant of *M. oligodon* in a pot survived the winter of 1963 without damage. They are rather lax climbers and do best when scrambling through shrubs, so that if they are to be given wall protection they will still do best if allowed to clamber over some other wall shrub or climber. The plants are all evergreen.

Mutisia clematis This is one of the more vigorous species and may reach a height of 20 ft or more. The nodding daisy-like flowers are bright orange in colour and are produced from June until September. This has proved one of the hardier species and is well worth a place in any garden. A large plant covered with these orange-scarlet daisies is a breath-taking sight.

Mutisia decurrens This is less vigorous than the last species, although it may reach a height of 12 ft. It has orange daisies that are up to 5 in. across, larger than those of *M. clematis*, which are usually about 2 in. wide. This seems more difficult to induce to grow well than most of the other species, although it is the best-known of them. Like so many Chilean plants it requires a cool, moist and shady root-run, but this can be said of all the species. It appears slightly happier on acid soil.

Mutisia ilicifolia Owing to its dark green, leathery, spiny leaves, this is known as the Holly-leaved Mutisia. It grows to about 10 ft and has pinky-mauve flowers about 2½ in. across. Like the other species, these are produced throughout the summer. *M. ilicifolia* will put up with quite a lot of frost and is well worth its wall-space. Indeed all the species are worth trying, owing to their long flowering season.

Mutisia oligodon This is a weak grower and likes to scramble about horizontally rather than climb straight up. The leaves resemble those of the last species, although they are far smaller and the rather small flowers are a delightful soft pink colour.

Mutisia retusa This can reach 15 ft, although it does not usually get quite so high and has agreeable pink flowers about 2½ in. across. This is one of the few species that can be relied upon to set seed outside in this country and it may well prove to be the hardiest of all the species.

Their reputation for tenderness has stopped people from planting these attractive climbers as frequently as their long flowering season and showy blooms suggest that they should be. I would like to suggest that they be tried more frequently. Most gardens have some position which is reasonably sheltered and a plant that will survive at Inverness is evidently not frost-tender in the usual sense of the term. Seed is, unfortunately, not usually available, otherwise the ideal would be to raise a number of seedlings and try them out in various positions. Cuttings of half-ripened wood are said to root easily and this would be an easier way of increasing the plants. When small they can be given winter protection and if the stock is then increased, they can be tried out in various promising looking situations. They are certainly worth the trouble that this involves.

PARTHENOCISSUS

As has already been mentioned **P. vitacea (inserta)** has tendrils without the adhesive disks that characterize the other species in cultivation. In appearance it is similar to *P. quinquefolia*, with five leaflets radiating from the centre, but those of *P. vitacea* are somewhat larger (in the var. *macrophylla*, they may be 8 in. long and 4 in. across) and a brighter green. They turn the same brilliant colour in the autumn. There is a var. *laciniata* with smaller leaves that are deeply toothed and present an elegant appearance.

PASSIFLORA

There is only one hardy Passion Flower and that is **P. caerulea.** This has been hybridized with the greenhouse species *P. raddiana* and *P. racemosa* and these hybrids are hardy in sheltered districts. Indeed it is claimed for a recent cross with *P. racemosa* that the hybrid is hardier than *P. caerulea* itself, but the plant has only just been introduced into cultivation and that remains to be proved.

P. caerulea has blue flowers with a white centre which are about 4 in. across and have the very elaborate sexual organs in which the early missionaries in S.America saw the instruments of the crucifixion. Although it must be regarded as a rather doubtful doer in cold districts, even with wall protection, it has been seen thriving in situations that would seem most unpromising and could be tried in all but the very coldest. It is indifferent as to soil, but a rich soil is apt to induce excessive growth at the expense of flowers and if your soil is too rich, it is as well to incorporate plenty of grit or gravel in the soil when planting the Passion Flower. Although a very severe frost may cut the plant to the ground, it will throw up fresh growths from the rootstock. The Passion Flower will not produce any blooms until it is quite sizeable and will then give a display from June until September. In hot summers the flowers are followed by egg-shaped orange fruits. The plant should not be pruned at all until it has started to flower, as any pruning will only encourage further leaf growth. When the plant does start to blossom, there is no objection to cutting back the leading shoots by about a one third of their length. This is usually done in early spring. There is a white form, *P. caerulea* 'Constance Elliott', which is extremely attractive.

One usually needs plenty of room to grow the Passion Flower, but if the roots can be confined in some way, the plant will be more restrained. It will do better with wall protection and must not be allowed to dry out at any time.

VITIS

The Vines are all rather vigorous climbers and, with the exception of *V. striata*, they are all deciduous. The majority are grown for their leaves alone, which are often large and imposing, usually attractively shaped and which generally turn good colours in the autumn before falling. The fruit is often attractive, but whether it is produced or not depends on the season. Most of the species can be propagated by 'eyes'. These are sections of the previous year's growth, cut so that only one bud is present. These are laid in soil and given gentle heat, when the bud will enlarge and start growing, while roots appear underneath.

If large trees or shrubs are available through which the vines can wander no pruning is necessary, but if they are grown on walls or posts or pergolas, they must be rigorously pruned. This entails shortening the main new growths by two thirds of their length and cutting out all laterals as close to the main stem as possible. This operation is best carried out in early winter. If this is not done the plant soon gets out of control and you are faced with an inextricable tangle, probably taking up far more room than you require. If they are grown against a wall or on a pergola it will be necessary to train some of the laterals horizontally, which means that you will have to tie them in to the required positions. Once you have laid out a good framework, you know that your vine will cover a large area. You will still have to prune yearly, but no further tying in will be necessary. Vines are greedy plants and enjoy a good soil, but they will give a good account of themselves whatever the soil may be. They are all hardy so far as winter frost is concerned, but, like so many shrubs, the young growth may be cut back by late spring frosts. With established plants this does not matter, as they will speedily produce fresh growths. With young plants, which are not yet established the damage may be fatal, so it is wise to be able to give such plants protection. Since they are pruned hard back the first year they are received, this is not difficult.

Vitis amurensis This is a vigorous climber with leaves that may be a foot long and 10 in. across. These leaves are deeply 3 or 5 lobed and turn crimson and dark purple in the autumn. The young shoots are reddish in colour and appear silky. The underside of the leaves is downy.

Vitis coignetiae This species cannot be propagated by eyes, but only by seeds or layers. It is the most vigorous of all the species in cultivation and must be allowed ample room. It is at its best growing up and over a large tree. This is a very imposing plant with its huge leaves that may be a foot long and 10 in. across. The leaves are roundish and only slightly lobed. The young shoots are covered with greyish down, but the underside of the leaves are clothed with a rusty-brown felt. The fruit is quite sizeable on the rare occasions when it is formed and is black with a bluish bloom. The plant is extremely brilliant in the autumn. In the best forms the leaves turn bright scarlet and even in the less good forms the leaves will turn pink and crimson. It must be realized that this plant needs plenty of room and no amount of pruning will turn it into a plant of moderate dimensions.

Vitis davidii (armata) Although vigorous enough, this is not quite so overpowering as the last species. The young shoots are covered with spiny bristles, which tend to disappear as the wood matures. The leaves are heart-shaped with a long slender point and are toothed around the edges. In mature plants they may reach 10 in. in length and 8 in. in width, but they are generally somewhat smaller. The small grapes are black or, in the var. *cyanocarpa*, blue and are said to have a pleasant flavour. Again the main season of beauty is the autumn, when the leaves will turn a very brilliant red.

Vitis flexuosa The plant in cultivation is the var. *parviflora*. This is probably the best species for growing on walls as it is a slender climber and not too vigorous. The leaves do not exceed 3 in. in length and are more or less heart-shaped. The upper side is a bronzy-green colour and the underside is purple. The autumn colour is not so startling as in some species, but to offset that the leaves are considerably more attractive during the summer than most of the others.

Vitis labrusca Although this is in cultivation, it is not among the most attractive species. It does, however, bear fruit quite often and some people find this palatable. Others complain of its 'foxy' flavour and in its native U.S.A. it is known as the Fox Grape. The leaves are rather thick and may reach 7 in. in length and width. They are roundish and may be three-lobed or completely unlobed. The young shoots are very woolly. The leaves at first have a whitish down on the underside, but this turns a rusty colour as the leaves mature. The leaves colour in the autumn, but by no means so brilliantly as the other species discussed.

Vitis piasezkii The name is enough to prevent anyone growing this attractive and not too vigorous vine. Like *Parthenocissus tricuspidata* one plant will bear leaves of different shapes. Some are composed of 3 or 5 leaflets, while others are a deeply-lobed oval in shape. The young shoots are covered with reddish down and this adheres all the time to the leaf stalks. The plant colours brilliantly in the autumn.

Vitis pulchra (flexuosa major of gardens**)** No one knows whence this plant came and it may possibly be of hybrid origin. It is rather vigorous with reddish shoots and young leaves. These leaves are roundish-ovate and may reach a length and width of 6 in. They may be slightly 3-lobed and are coarsely toothed. The mature leaves are a shining green on top, but the underside is covered with grey down. In the autumn the leaves turn blood red or deep purple.

Vitis riparia (odoratissima, vulpina) This is unusual among the vines, in that it is not grown so much for the sake of the leaves as for the fragrance of its flowers. These are produced in June and have the same fragrance as Mignonette. Apart from that, it is a vigorous climber with leaves that are roughly heart-shaped, with a finely tapered point and coarse teeth on the edges. The leaves may reach 8 in. in length and are a shining green. The autumn tints are less conspicuous than in some other species, but are not to be despised.

Vitis (Cissus) striata (Ampelopsis sempervirens) A plant of various names among which the botanically correct *Cissus striata* is the one least likely to be found in any plant catalogue. It is the only evergreen among the vines and also the only species, among those discussed, of which there is the slightest doubt as to its hardiness. In cold districts it is advisable to give it the protection of a wall, although in its native Chile it grows over shrubs and bushes. It is a slender plant and not very vigorous as a climber, with leaves composed of five leaflets. These are very slender, obovate in shape and up to 1½ in. long and ¾ in. across; the whole compound leaf is not more than 3 in. across. The fruits, when produced, are reddish purple in colour. The late W. J. Bean, in his classic *Trees and Shrubs Hardy in the British Isles*, describes this as 'a very elegant plant, luxuriantly leafy and with beautifully cut leaves'. It is rather a plant for the south and west and displays itself best when scrambling over a large shrub. However its host must be chosen with care as it will probably be damaged by having an evergreen climber growing over it. The plant is also useful for disguising unsightly erections, whether they be sheds or some other unpleasaunce, to borrow Messrs Sellar and Yeatman's marvellous term.

Vitis thunbergii This is one of the less vigorous vines and frequently fails to ripen all its wood in this country. Where it is being pruned this is of no account and even when it is growing in a position where pruning is not necessary, it should do no actual harm, although it means that there is a certain amount of dead wood about and this may attract fungus diseases. Owing to its deeply lobed leaves—they are either 3 or 5 lobed—which bear a resemblance to those of the fig, the plant is sometimes referred to as the Fig-leaved Vine. The leaves may reach a width of 6 in. and a length of 8 in. and they have a rusty-brown tomentum on the underside. The grapes are in small bunches and are black with a purple bloom. This is one of the more brilliant autumn colourers and, owing to its more moderate growth, is the obvious choice where the really vigorous vines such as *amurensis* and *coignetiae* are too rampant.

Vitis vinifera This is the usual grape vine, from which all our wine and dessert grapes come. Many will not fruit satisfactorily in this climate, but a large number of varieties are available which do fruit satisfactorily. However our concern is not with the fruiting varieties, but with those which make attractive garden plants. These are all hardy and are capable of making very large plants, if such are needed and must, in any case, be given a sizeable space to fill, even if their growth is to be restricted. The fruiting cultivars often show good autumn tints, but they need special treatment and will not fruit so satisfactorily if given the treatment that is best for climbers. When one thinks of the thousands of years that the vine has been cultivated, it is quite surprising that so few ornamental varieties have evolved.

(*a*) var. *apiifolia* (*laciniosa*) This, the so-called Parsley Vine, has its leaves deeply incised and they make a very attractive picture, when the plant is in full leaf. It produces small black grapes and does not colour so much as some other vines in the autumn, although it usually gives some display of colour.
(*b*) var. *incana*. This has rather small leaves, which may be unlobed or which may have three lobes. The whole plant, including the leaves, is covered with a grey cobwebby down, which gives the plant an unusual appearance, although not one that is particularly attractive on its own. However in combination with contrasting leaves, or with a clematis growing among the grey leaves, some effective results can be obtained. It would also look well growing through a purple-leaved Prunus. The plant is sometimes known as the Dusty Miller Vine. I have never heard of it bearing fruit, but there is no reason to suppose that it doesn't.
(*c*) var. *purpurea*. The Dyer's Grape is one of the most brilliant of all purple-leaved shrubs and there is no climber to compare with it. The young leaves are a beautiful claret colour and they deepen to a dark purple and may turn crimson before they fall. Unless you are one of those who detest plants with purple leaves, this is an unusually attractive vine, which can be kept within certain bounds by yearly pruning.

The above are all the vines which are commonly available, but as one reads through the descriptions of some that have dropped out of cultivation one finds one or two that would seem to merit reintroduction. Outstanding among these from its description is *V. bicolor*. This has lobed leaves that may reach 12 in. in each direction with a blue-white underside. It is evidently a plant to grow on a pergola or an arch, so that the brilliant undersurface of the leaves can be appreciated. It would not be much use on a wall.

Since it grows as far north as Niagara Falls, there need be no doubt about its hardiness in this country. The young shoots also show this blue-white coloration and the plant sounds extremely striking. Let us hope that it will soon be available.

Although vines will grow in any soil, they are at their most vigorous when they have a long root-run which will not dry out in the summer. Although in the wild they grow up trees, they will grow quite happily without their roots being shaded as many acres of vineyards show. They are greedy feeders and liable to impoverish the soil for some distance round their trunks. In this way they present a certain problem for the gardener. If he manures around the trunk, in order to grow other flowers at the base, he is liable to provoke a vigorous plant to an excessive display of growth. If he does no such thing, he is not able to grow plants very well round the base. The ideal is to have the roots of the vines extend under the lawn, which can be kept going by top-dressing. This may not always be possible. If it is not, it is best to select shallow-rooting plants to put in the vicinity of vines, as their own roots are normally some little distance from the surface.

II HERBACEOUS TENDRILLED CLIMBERS

Among these may be found both annual and perennial plants and also what is, I would imagine, the solitary example of a biennial climber. Although a large number of the Leguminosae, the Pea family, employ this method of climbing, there are not a great number in cultivation and the list could easily be enlarged if some plants that were formerly cultivated were reintroduced. Some of the plants like the Clematis, use their leaf-stalks as tendrils and outstanding among these is the Tropaeolum. As one might expect from plants that have to make all their growth in the spring and summer, they are not particularly vigorous with one or two exceptions. As a general rule one may assume that they will not much exceed 6 ft in height; exceptions will be noted when we come to consider the plants separately. As they start each year from ground level they will need some fine twiggy growth or support to act as a host. Many will be happy growing among low hedges and a hedge is really the most suitable place for the larger *Lathyrus* spp. It is worthwhile loosening the soil to some depth, even for the annuals, as anyone who has ever grown prize Sweet Peas will realize. Manure is always welcomed by nearly every plant, but it is not really necessary, unless you have ample to spare. Very few gardeners do in fact have much more than their compost heaps, unless they happen to have a farm as well as a garden. In any case most of these herbaceous and annual climbers will do well without any artificial aids, provided that the soil is loosened sufficiently to give them a good long root run. With these herbaceous plants it is not always so necessary for the roots to be in the shade; it appears to be essential with *Tropaeolum speciosum*, but most of the others will thrive even in situations where they get a lot of hot sun, provided that they are able to get their roots well down. There are one or two exceptions which will be noted as we come to them and, in any case, it is always better to place them where they do have their roots in the shade. Since they will not flower until they have emerged from this shade it is best to plant them where they can soon get into the light.

ADLUMIA

This is a monotypic genus, although there seems still some doubt as to whether its specific name is **fungosa** or **cirrhosa** and it can be met with under either name. This is, so far as I know, the only biennial climber; though there is always the possibility that this may reflect my ignorance rather than its uniqueness.

The plant is a member of the Fumitory family and comes from North America. It seems to do best in a rather light, peaty, acid soil. Seed is sown in the spring and the plants put in a shady or partly shady position as soon as they are large enough. The plant is not too happy at root disturbance and there might be much to be said in favour of sowing the seeds where they are wanted to grow. During its first year the plant makes a rosette of very attractive fern-like leaves that may be 10 in. across. It passes the winter as a rosette plant and in the following spring starts to throw up one or more climbing stems which attach themselves to their host by means of their leaf-stalks. They can ascend as high as 6 ft and need a rather twiggy support. The flowers appear in little racemes in the leaf axils and are generally rosy-pink, although white forms are known. In shape they resemble the popular *Dicentra formosa* and are nearly the same size. The plant is very attractive with its ferny leaves and curiously shaped flowers, but it has one disadvantage. The seed-pods form within the dead flowers, which never fall off, so that the lower part of the plant looks somewhat unsightly. The plant insists on a shady position and does not like bright sunshine for long periods even when it is flowering. It is tolerant of severe frosts, as one would expect of a plant coming from the northern parts of N.America, but it is sometimes intolerant of the excessive damp that our winters may produce, and in badly drained soil winter losses are not uncommon. For some reason the plant is listed as being half-hardy, but this cannot be true in the normal sense, as, otherwise, the plant would be extinct in its natural habitat. Certainly in my own garden it has proved immune to any frost, including one night of zero fahrenheit, but plants in badly-drained situations where the soil is heavy have not done well the first year and died off in the winter. Where conditions are to its liking it will seed itself naturally. In spite of wanting a well-drained soil, it likes this to be reasonably damp and will require watering during prolonged dry spells.

COBAEA

A genus of climbing shrubs belonging to the Polemoniaceae, not a family with which one tends to associate climbers. Its most well-known garden genus is Polemonium itself, Jacob's Ladder, and Phlox. All the species sound rather attractive, but only one is usually available. This is **Cobaea scandens,** which will act as a perennial in a greenhouse, but which is generally treated as a half-hardy annual.

The rather large seeds are said to germinate most rapidly if they are inserted on edge in their soil and they require a certain amount of heat to germinate (about 65°F). They should be sown as early in the year as possible and, if you have no greenhouse, will probably be happy on the window-sill of your warmest room. As you cannot put the plants out until there is no risk of spring frosts, it will probably be necessary to pot the seedlings on singly. This is a plant that requires the warmest position available when put outside and will thrive on a south wall, although other elevations may prove satisfactory. I doubt if much success would be obtained on north or east walls; but success would probably come from south-east facing walls and possibly from north-west ones. The plant has tendrils and climbs very rapidly, often reaching 15 ft during its one season. The large flowers suggest a rather curious daffodil as the tubular mauve or greeny-white flowers are subtended by a green saucer of sepals and these flowers are very popular for exotic-looking floral arrangements. This is a very suitable plant for training up a wall shrub, or up some early-flowering climber. Being of only annual duration it will not cause any damage and will lend interest at a time when it might otherwise be lacking. The plants continue to flower until the frosts come, but the time that they will start depends on how advanced the plants are, before they are planted out. They seldom start to flower before they are 5 ft high.

CORYDALIS

Corydalis claviculata is a weak annual climber of rather weedy appearance, with small pale yellow flowers and elegant fumitory-like leaves. The plant is occasionally found wild in this country and is too weak to train on to a shrub, but it will climb up some herbaceous plant. The plant is not particularly attractive, but has a quiet charm of its own, which some people will like.

CUCURBITA

The various ornamental gourds are tendrilled climbers, although it is not often that one sees them climbing to any great extent. However they will grow happily on trellis work and are useful for training over old stumps and rather small unsightly objects. Although *C. ficifolia* is perennial in sufficiently warm climates, it should probably be treated as a half-hardy annual in this country. The R.H.S. Dictionary of Gardening does suggest that it is hardy, without actually stating so. Most of the ornamental gourds belong to the same species, *C. pepo*, from which all the various Squash and Vegetable Marrows have been developed and their leaves do suggest the kitchen garden. If looked at dispassionately, they are really rather handsome and the yellow flowers are quite ornamental. The gourds themselves are not particularly noticeable until the plant is well advanced and they do not add a great deal to the ornament of the garden, although they are much used for winter decoration in the home.

The seeds are very large and can be sown singly in pots in gentle heat, about the beginning of April and they are planted out as soon as the risk of spring frosts has gone. They can also be planted directly in the soil in May, but they will be later coming into fruit. As they are somewhat large coarse plants, they need something substantial on which to climb. They might well damage a delicate shrub, and trellis work is usually recommended. If there is some sort of screen between the flower and vegetable sections of the garden, this would seem to be the ideal situation.

Cucurbita ficifolia (melanosperma) This is a vigorous climber with large marbled leaves, that are 5 lobed. The leaves themselves are rounded in shape. The fruits are about a foot long and are white with black seeds inside. This is the only perennial species in the genus, but, outside a greenhouse, it would be wisest to regard it as a half-hardy annual.

Cucurbita pepo This has been in cultivation for so long, that no one is certain whence the original wild species was collected, although tropical S.America would seem the most probable locality. Since one of its forms is the popular Vegetable Marrow, there would seem no need to describe the plant, but various cultivars have been raised for the sake of their ornamental fruits. These can either be purchased mixed or selected forms can be purchased under such names as 'Turban' 'dish-cloth gourd' 'pear-shaped gourd' etc.

Other gourds will be found under *Lagenaria* and *Momordica*, although the last-named will only do well in a hot season.

All Cucurbitas like a rich soil and plenty of moisture when they are growing well. Although better plants are obtained by starting in heat, they do seem to experience a slight check when planted out. Incidentally it is as well to harden them off for ten days before planting them out into the soil. Plants coming straight from indoors into the ground are very soft and succulent and slugs will travel a long way to eat them. Once planted out, there may be, as I have said, some slight check and until growth is resumed too much water should not be given. Of course there is nothing you can do if it rains, but if it is dry, it is best to give a good watering when planting out and no more until growth is observed.

ECCREMOCARPUS

Eccremocarpus scaber is a member of the Bignonia family and is treated as a half-hardy annual, although it quite often proves perennial, particularly in mild districts, and is liable to produce self-sown seedlings in colder areas, which suggests that there is no need to treat it as half-hardy, even when treated as an annual. However, if the seedlings are started in heat you will get a better plant the first year. It is a rapid grower, seldom reaching more than 8 ft in height and has delicate pinnate leaves and racemes of tubular flowers, each about 1 in. long and orange in colour. Yellow and reddish-purple forms are known, but are not always easy to obtain. This is a plant that can happily be allowed to wander over another climber or a wall plant. If the plant does survive the winter, it shows itself to be evergreen and develops a woody base. It flowers continuously from July to October, never making any very large display and, as has been noted, is liable to seed itself around. It is a rather quiet plant, but useful owing to its long flowering season.

LAGENARIA

This is the Bottle Gourd, with long bottle-shaped fruits of varying size and form. Fruits up to 6 ft long have been recorded, and the form called 'leucantha longissima' will normally produce 3-ft bottles. Although some forms are listed under the name 'leucantha', they are all selected forms of **L. vulgaris.** They require treatment similar to *Cucurbita*, although they may need rather more heat to get germination. Unlike *Cucurbita* the flowers of *Lagenaria* are white not yellow. Like all the *Cucurbitaceae* a single plant bears both male and female flowers and sometimes artificial fertilization is necessary. As a general rule a number of male flowers appear before any female ones, but more male flowers will be produced later. Very occasionally *Lagenaria* will produce plants of one sex only, so it is as well to grow a number, in case this unusual event should occur.

LATHYRUS

This is a fairly large genus of the *Leguminosae* with pea-like flowers and which includes both annuals and perennials. A number of these seem to have been temporarily lost to cultivation, but I am mentioning some of the more attractive here, in the hopes that a demand will create a further supply. The plants are not fussy about their soil, although they will do better if it is not too impacted. They like to be able to get their roots well down. The perennial species prefer to have their roots cool and in the shade, but this is not essential. The annuals can be planted in full sun, but should be kept moist in their early stages. Drought at this point will prevent good development. By no means all the species are climbing; some are herbaceous perennials of quite moderate growth.

Lathyrus cirrhosus A fairly vigorous perennial, with rather narrow leaves and peduncles of rosy-purple pea-like flowers. It is not altogether easy to distinguish this plant from the other 'Everlasting Peas', *Ll. latifolius* and *rotundifolius*, although they appear quite distinct if grown alongside each other.

Lathyrus grandiflorus This annual species has dropped out of cultivation and should be reintroduced. It has its leaflets in single pairs and large deep pink flowers in sprays of 2 or 3. It is a native of Southern Europe and should not be difficult to re-establish in cultivation. It is in some ways more showy than the not dissimilar *L. tingitanus*, which is still available.

Lathyrus latifolius This is the most widely grown of the perennial species and is what most people mean when they speak of the Everlasting Pea. It may reach 10 ft each season in a favourable situation, although it is usually less. The normal colour is a rosy-purple, but there are some forms that are a better, clearer, red and a white form that is, perhaps, the most attractive of them all. The plant is best propagated by seed and if plants are purchased, they are best when not very large, as the plant resents root disturbance and may sulk for a year or so if moved when too large. The roots also descend to great depths, so that it is not easy to move mature plants without destroying most of the roots. The flowers appear in August.

Lathyrus magellanicus Why Lord Anson's Pea is no longer in cultivation is hard to understand, as it is very distinct from all the other lathyrus. It is a vigorous climber with many-flowered peduncles of bluish pea-like flowers that are produced in succession from mid-June until September. There has never been any suggestion that the plant is not hardy and one wonders why it should have dropped out of cultivation.

Lathyrus odoratus This is the most popular of all the species and one of the most popular of all garden plants. You may not recognize it under this name, as it is never referred to. It is, of course, the Sweet Pea. The original wild plant, which is very attractive with its reddish purple flowers and very strong perfume comes from southern Italy, but is not in cultivation.

Lathyrus pubescens This is the only species to be mentioned here that is not reliably hardy. It is a native of Chile and Uruguay and might be killed in a severe winter. It can also be distinguished by the fact that the stems and leaves are somewhat hairy. The flowers are lavender in colour and so give a colour that no other species can supply. It is probably best grown in a sheltered situation and the young growths should be given protection as they come through in the spring. Even so a prolonged spell of severe frost might destroy the roots. The plant is easily raised from seed, although it may be three years before flowers are seen.

Lathyrus rotundifolius This is a handsome everlasting pea, distinguished by its rounded leaflets. It is as vigorous as *L. latifolius*, but some forms have a rather clearer red in the flowers and are to be preferred on that score. Unfortunately this good colour is not universal and it is necessary to raise a large number of seedlings and then discard the unsatisfactory ones.

Lathyrus sativus (azureus) This is an annual climber and seems to be no longer in cultivation. Since it is the only species with blue flowers, and quite a brilliant blue at that, it seems a pity. It is rather more slender than the other annuals described and it bears only a single flower on each stem. This is about the same size as that of a garden Pea and, as mentioned, a good bright blue in colour. On occasion it appears to have been called the Chickling Pea. It is a plant that requires to be grown in a clump to give of its best effect. Single plants do not have sufficient flowers out at a time.

Lathyrus tingitanus This is rather a handsome annual, which will reach a height of some 6 ft or more. The flowers are about the size of those of a Sweet Pea and the most usual form has a rosy-purple standard and a crimson keel. I have seen a form that was glowing crimson all over in the wild, but I do not think that it is in cultivation.

Lathyrus tuberosus This is a sprawler rather than a climber, although the leaves are furnished with tendrils and it will pull itself a short distance off the ground if given some twigs to support it. Although a most spectacular plant, it must be regarded as rather a menace, as once established it seems to be ineradicable. There are always a few of the small tubers left in the ground. However if space can be found, there are few plants more brilliant in flower. It spreads rapidly and it is probably safest to try and contain the roots in some way. The flowers appear from July onwards and are a very brilliant crimson-carmine. The individual flowers are small, but they are produced in great profusion. I do not know what the plant described under this name in the R.H.S. Dictionary is, but it is not *L. tuberosus*. The plant is found naturalized in a few places in this country and has been known for so long around Fyfield in Essex, that it is known as the Fyfield Pea.

MAURANDIA

In this genus are a couple of climbers, which would be perennial in the greenhouse, but which are treated as half-hardy annuals. They are natives of Mexico and some heat is needed to get germination sufficiently early for the plants to flower out of doors. When grown out of doors they are not particularly vigorous and it is improbable that they will exceed 6 ft in height; they may not even reach it. The flowers are large and tubular and are various shades of purple, pink and white.

Maurandia barclaiana A fairly vigorous climber in the greenhouse, but comparatively restrained when grown outside. Like all the genus, it climbs by wrapping its leaf-stalk around its host and so needs some twiggy support. The tubular flowers are generally about 2 in. long and are deep purple, dark rose, pale rose or white in colour.

Maurandia erubescens This differs from the last species in its more triangular leaves and in its larger flowers, which are generally 3 in. long. The flowers are rose-pink while the tube is white with some markings on the inside.

Maurandia lophospermum (Lophosperum scandens) This is very like the last-named species, but has reddish-purple flowers and the white tube is dotted on the outside.
There is really very little to chose between the various species; they are all attractive with their foxglove like flowers.

MOMORDICA

This is a tropical genus of the *Cucurbitaceae*, with attractive gourd-like fruits, that split open when ripe and expose their ornamental seeds. Although they are said to fruit satisfactorily out of doors, I, personally, would regard their cultivation as somewhat hazardous. However as seed is available and not expensive, there is much to be said for having a go. The seeds need a minimum night temperature of 60°F to insure germination and should be started about the beginning of March. The plants must remain under cover until the end of May, when they are put out in as warm a situation as possible and given a light rich soil. They must not be allowed to dry out. Two species are available.

Momordica balsamina Known as the Balsam Apple, this climber, which is quite vigorous, has five-lobed shining leaves and yellow flowers that are spotted with brown. The fruits are egg-shaped, about the size of an apple, orange in colour and covered with warts. When the fruit is ripe, it splits open showing brilliant orange flesh among which the black seeds appear.

Momordica charantia This is the Balsam Pear and is larger in every way. The leaves are somewhat hairy and the flowers are yellow. The fruits are oblong and yellowish or copper-coloured. The seeds are white or pale brown and are attached to the flesh by bright scarlet arils.

As these plants are usually given warm greenhouse treatment, I should, perhaps emphasize again that their successful culture outside must be regarded as hazardous.

TROPAEOLUM

There are many very attractive plants among the nasturtiums, but some of the best have been lost to cultivation. Since these species mostly need cool greenhouse treatment, the loss is not severe as far as the present book is concerned. Of the climbing species that are available in gardens, there are three annuals and two perennials. The annual species will grow happily in any soil and since the seeds are very large, they can be planted individually. Although they will grow in shady situations they only flower freely in sunshine and can be planted in full sun without any worry. The perennial species need different treatment which will be discussed as we come to them.

Tropaeolum majus This is the common Nasturtium, which will grow and flower anywhere and seed itself around. Although treated as a hardy annual, it is frost tender and young plants can be killed by late spring frosts. Like all the species under consideration it climbs by means of its leaf-stalks and so some appropriate support must be provided. It has circular peltate leaves (i.e. the leaf-stalk joins the leaf at its centre) and a rounded flower with a long spur. The wild plant, which comes from Peru, had orange flowers, but nowadays, as a result of selection and hybridization with other species, it can be procured in all colours from yellow, through red and orange to scarlet. This, like the other annual species, does better in rather poor soil; if the soil is too rich they are liable to grow at the expense of flowers. They are sometimes attacked by Black Fly, in which case they must be sprayed with an appropriate insecticide. Cabbage White Butterflies will also lay their eggs on the leaves and there is a risk of caterpillars damaging the plants. However these can usually be sought out and removed by hand.

Tropaeolum peltophorum (lobbianum) Although similar in many ways to *T. majus*, this plant is slightly smaller, covered with fine down and has the lower petals attractively fringed. The flowers are mainly in red shades, but yellows have been recorded. It is not certain that the true species is still in cultivation, as it appears to have hybridized a lot with *T. majus*. However the plant still shows its attractive fringed flowers and is a more elegant plant than the last species.

Tropaeolum peregrinum (canariense) The Canary Creeper is attractive on account of its glaucous, grey-green 5-lobed leaves. The yellow flowers are neither so large nor so attractive as in the last two species. In the greenhouse this is a perennial, but it is always treated as a half-hardy annual. It always seems to me odd that this should have continued in cultivation, while so many more attractive plants have been lost. In spite of its synonym of *canariense*, this, like the whole genus, comes from S. America.

Tropaeolum speciosum Sometimes called the Flame Flower, this is an herbaceous perennial with a creeping rhizome. It is a Chilean plant and must have acid or neutral soil and a cool, moist shady root run. Where this plant thrives it is extremely effective. It appears to do better in the northern part of the country and various experts give quite contradictory instructions as to the best way of growing it. The most effective way would appear to be to obtain pot-grown plants and place them in what might be considered suitable positions. Some recommended planting the roots at least 9 in. deep, while others suggest that you lay the root on the surface, only burying the extremities. Although everyone agrees on the cool, shady root run, I know someone who has it growing up a Ceanothus on a south-facing wall. Once the plant has got established, it will run about under ground until it finds the situation it prefers. One suggestion that is frequently put forward is to plant it on the shadiest side of a hedge (in my youth it had to be a Yew hedge) and encourage it to come up and climb through to the other side. It is worth every effort to encourage it to do well.

The plant itself has slender, twining stems that can reach to 10 ft in the season. The round leaves are divided into 6 leaflets, so as to give an attractive appearance, even before the flowers emerge. When these do they are about 1½ in. across and a reddish-scarlet in colour. They are produced over a long period from mid-June onwards. When a plant is well established and sending up numerous stems, it can wreath its host with a sheet of scarlet, which is breath-taking. It is only in the north that it seems able to do this. Plants in the south, although they may look most attractive, never seem to have the exuberance and floriferousness of those grown further north. The seeds have an attractive blue sheen, which gives a further attraction, when they are formed but this is not always to be relied upon.

Tropaeolum tuberosum The other perennial Tropaeolum, that can be grown out of doors, is of far easier culture, but there is sometimes some difficulty in obtaining flowers. At one time there appeared to be two clones in cultivation, one of which flowered well, while the other grew to excess and never produced flowers. Let us hope that this unsatisfactory clone has been discontinued. The plant has quite large yellow, purple-flushed tubers, which should be treated like dahlias and planted out in mid-May. An acid soil is to be preferred, but otherwise a rather poor soil suits the plant best and it should not be given the cool moist conditions that suit *T. speciosum.* On the contrary they should be planted in a warm and well-lit situation. The plant climbs to about 7 ft in the season and from July onwards produces single orange flowers that are held in a scarlet calyx, so that a bicolor effect is created. The plant does not produce a sheet of blossom like the Flame Nasturtium, but is of charm and interest over a long period. The lobed leaves are basically kidney-shaped and the stems and leaf-stalks are reddish. When frost cuts the growths down, the tubers should be lifted, as they will be found to have come very near the surface. In mild districts it is possible to replant them at once at a depth of 6 in. but, in colder localities they should be lifted and overwintered in a frost-free place. They should not dry out completely and they are best placed in soil or peat which is kept barely moist. Since there is always a large increase in the number of tubers, it is quite possible to replant some and store the rest. The tubers are, incidentally, edible and can be peeled and boiled as though they were Jerusalem Artichokes. I have never tried them, so cannot say if this is an advisable method of disposing of surplus tubers. They are more likely to be prized as gifts to fellow-gardeners. Seed is set with some freedom, but seems difficult to germinate.

A species one would like to see reintroduced, as it can be treated as a half-hardy annual, is **T. smithii,** which had bright orange-red, heavily fringed flowers. Its habitat is given simply as S. America, which is somewhat vague and it was introduced to cultivation as long ago as 1775. There are a number of other attractive sounding climbers, including the blue-flowered *T. azureum*, but these all require greenhouse treatment, or rather they would if they were still available.

5 Closer than a brother

By far the largest number of climbers ascend by twining round their hosts in a spiral. This habit of growth indicates that the plant will grow naturally among quite tall trees or shrubs, although the more feeble amongst them, such as *Convolvulus tenuissimus*, will be found growing among dwarf scrub. Indeed some of the convolvulus, like our native *C. arvensis*, are quite happy sprawling over the ground, although they will twine round anything that they meet. As with the plants in the last chapter, we shall meet with shrubs and herbaceous twiners.

If it is desired to lead these twiners into established trees, it is advisable to give them some form of rather slender support at the start. A tree trunk is rather too large an obstacle for a young plant. Of course, where the tree and the climber grow up together, this particular problem does not arise; instead you have the rather more serious one of the climber growing more rapidly than its host. In this case the host may be smothered and it is not a practice that I would encourage. Once your host is established, the twiner can be led into it up a cane, which is long enough to get it into the more slender branches, or it can be conducted up a rope attached high up in its host. If they are being grown on walls, they can be left to ramble over plastic mesh or some similar wire support. Annuals will be content with long canes. Although, like all climbers, they do best when their roots are in the shade and the root-run is cool and shady, there are some which will thrive without these conditions being provided.

I SHRUBBY TWINERS

There are a very large number of shrubby twiners, but not so many that are really attractive. It should be noted that all twiners have a recognized method of twining; some twine from right to left, while the others twine from left to right. It is as well to observe this, so that, if you have to assist the plant in its early stages, you will not offend against its nature.

ACTINIDIA

A genus of about 40 species, mainly found in China. They are all fairly vigorous and most of them are dioecious; one plant being male, while the other is female. As the fruits are sometimes ornamental, this is a pity. They like a rich loamy soil, but do not seem to mind as to whether it is acid or alkaline. They will not thrive on thin chalky soils, but this is due to the thinness, not the chalkiness, and if a good hole is excavated and filled with a suitable mixture, they will get away quite happily in the chalk. The two species with variegated leaves *Aa kolomikta* and *polygama* are said to have an extraordinary attraction for cats and should be protected when young, against their too enthusiastic attentions. There are quite a few species in cultivation, although only two, *chinensis* and *kolomikta* are popular.

Actinidia arguta This is a very vigorous climber, often reaching in its native China to the tops of tall trees. It is also one of the few species with hermaphrodite flowers, so that, in theory, fruits will appear on a single plant. It is, however, chiefly grown as a foliage plant as the flowers are small and white and the fruits are greenish-yellow berries about 1 in. long. However, although the flowers are small, they are fragrant and being produced in clumps of three are more conspicuous than the description would suggest. The leaves, which are borne on reddish stalks, are ovate, up to 5 in long and nearly as wide and are a dark lustrous green in colour. There is a variety *cordifolia*, in which the base of the leaf is markedly heart-shaped and the leaf stalks are purple and hairy.

Actinidia chinensis The Chinese Gooseberry. This is one of the most popular species, with quite large attractive flowers and ornamental and edible fruits. Some plants are hermaphrodite, but most are unisexual, so that it is advisable to obtain two sexed plants if possible, if fruit is desired. This again is a vigorous plant, capable of reaching 30 ft. There is a distinct difference between the flowering shoots, which emerge from year old wood, and sterile branches. The stems of the sterile shoots are covered with shaggy red hairs, whereas those of the flowering shoots are only downy. Leaves on the sterile shoots are heart-shaped, up to 8 in. long and 7 in. wide, with the stems and the underside of the midrib and the major veins covered with the same shaggy red hairs as the branchlets themselves. The fertile shoot leaves are smaller and nearly circular, up to 4 in. long and 3 in. wide. These fertile shoots bear in August, flowers $1\frac{1}{2}$ in. across in small clusters. These are white when they emerge, but fade to a buff colour. The fruits are shaped like a gooseberry and are covered with hairs. They are a dark red-brown. The fruits are somewhat insipid, but sufficiently popular to be offered for sale by the more enterprising greengrocers.

Actinidia coriacea. This is a fairly vigorous climber, capable of reaching to 25 ft and the least hardy of those in cultivation. The leaves, which are leathery as the name suggests, are lance-shaped, up to 5 in. long and 1½ in. across and are toothed at the edges. The small flowers, about ½ in. across are produced in groups of 3–5 in the leaf axils and are reddish in colour. They appear in early summer and, if plants of both sexes are present, the female flowers are followed by small egg-shaped brownish fruits.

Actinidia giraldii This is a vigorous climber, akin in many ways to *A. arguta*. The plant has broadly elliptic or ovate leaves that will reach a length of 5 in. and a width of 3 in. These leaves are slightly hairy on the underside. The white flowers are small, in clusters in the leaf axils. This plant was only introduced to cultivation in 1933, but does not seem to be outstandingly attractive.

Actinidia kolomikta This is, probably, the most popular species on account of its colourful leaves. It is far less vigorous than the species so far described, although it can eventually reach a height of 15 ft. It usually rarely exceeds 10 ft. The leaves are more or less heart-shaped and parts of this leaf will be variegated pink or white. The amount of variegation varies from leaf to leaf; some will be wholly coloured, while only the tips of other leaves will be affected. This variegation develops after the leaf has expanded fully. Male plants appear to show more of this and it also appears that a warm situation will also encourage this variegation. For this reason it is often at its best trained against a wall or fence. The flowers are small and white in groups of 1–3 in the leaf axils and the fruits are quite palatable and yellowish in colour. This is one of the two species which have great fascination for cats, so that young plants must be protected.

Actinidia melanandra A tall climber with pointed oblong leaves up to 4 in. long and 1½ in. across. The white flowers are quite sizeable in the male plants, the female flowers are smaller, but are produced in a short spike. The egg-shaped fruits are slightly over 1 in. long and are covered with a purple bloom. This is quite a useful plant, where a vigorous climber is needed, but it is not so attractive as *A. chinensis*.

Actinidia polygama This is in many ways similar to *A. kolomikta* and has the same attraction for cats. It is slightly more vigorous, but will not exceed 20 ft in height. The stems branch frequently and it is not long before the plant is a tangled mass. The leaves are elliptical, up to 5 in. long and the stalks and the underside of the leaf veins are bristly. The variegation, which is either pale yellow or silver-white, is very much more marked in the male plants and these are accordingly the more desirable. The pink shades, that appear in *A. kolomikta* are not recorded from this species. On the other hand it is more vigorous than *A. kolomikta*. The flowers, too, are slightly larger and have an attractive fragrance. It grows more suitably on a tree or large shrub than on a wall and is thus suitable for positions for which the other variegated species would be too small.

Actinidia purpurea This is related to *A. arguta*, although it is less overwhelming, not exceeding 25 ft in height. It has oblong-oval leaves that may be 5 in. long and flowers in small clusters. These are white and a little over $\frac{1}{2}$ in. across. It gets its specific name from the inch-long purple fruits that are produced when plants of both sexes are in the garden. Since few of us have enough room to accommodate two vigorous climbers, for the sake of the fruits of one, it is not liable to be found in fruit very often.

AKEBIA

A genus of two species of vigorous twining shrubs belonging to the *Lardizabalaceae*, a family close to the Berberis family. A rather deep loamy soil is best for these plants; but they are indifferent as to whether it is acid or aklaline. In most parts of the country they are deciduous, but in mild localities they may carry their leaves through the winter, only dropping them when the new ones emerge. The plants are monoecious, having the male and female flowers on the same inflorescence. The numerous small male flowers are at the end of the spike, while two or three larger female flowers are nearest the stem and are much larger. They are best used on trees or trained over pillars, rather than grown on walls. The flowers are not very conspicuous and are of a curious chocolate colour, and those of *A. quinata* give out a spicy scent that is very pervasive. After hot summers the attractive fruits are seen, but they cannot be relied upon to be produced regularly.

Akebia lobata (trifoliata) The leaves are composed of three stalked leaflets, with the stalk of the centre leaflet three times as long as those of the two laterals. The individual leaflets are ovate and up to 4 in. long. The flower spikes appear in April, as the leaves are unfurling. The spike is a pendulous raceme up to 5 in. long with a large number of small male flowers and usually only two female flowers. If these flowers are not damaged by frost and if the summer is sufficiently warm, the violet-coloured sausage-shaped fruits will be developed. These are up to 5 in. long and when fully ripe they split open to reveal the black seeds embedded in white flesh.

Akebia quinata In this species the leaf is composed of five, short-stalked leaflets of a particularly attractive green, rather reminiscent of the colour of young Maidenhair Fern leaves. The flowers, that emerge at the end of April or in early May, are on shorter racemes than in the last species, but they exhale a delicious fragrance. The individual leaflets are oblong-oval and about 2–3 in. long and the plant has a very attractive appearance with these delicate-looking leaves. When the fruits are produced they are egg-shaped and rarely more than 3 in. long, smaller than those of *A. lobata* and they are more purple in colour.

Both the akebias are attractive foliage plants that look as though they should be tender. In point of fact they appear to be bone-hardy and can be recommended where sufficient space is available.

ARISTOLOCHIA

The plants in this genus offer a curious mixture of extremely vigorous and rather feeble climbers. The plants are known as Dutchman's Pipe, owing to the curious shape of the flowers, which are curved and tubular with an expanded end. There are tropical species where the flowers are very large and conspicuous, but those of the hardy species are rather small and not very noticeable. They have a rather sinister appearance, which gives them a great attraction to some people, including the writer. The two evergreen species are natives of the Mediterranean and do best in a rather stony alkaline soil. The two deciduous American species are happiest with a loamy soil and slightly prefer it to be acid, although they are not really fussy.

Aristolochia altissima This is an evergreen species from the Mediterranean region, where it grows in maquis country and scrambles up plants such as cistus. Against a wall it can reach a height of 10 ft, but is usually rather less than this. It has shining green leaves, which are slightly waved and only about 2½ in. long. The yellowish-brown flowers appear on slender stalks from the upper leaf axils. They are about 1½ in. long and have the characteristic shape of the genus, which has flowers adapted to trap flies in the flower, so as to ensure pollination. In a severe winter the plant may be cut to the ground but if established, will always throw up fresh growths. This probably does best if planted among low shrubs, which will protect the lower portions of the plant and over which it can ramble. It is evidently not a plant for cold localities and it, like the other species, belongs to the type of plant that are always described as curious rather than beautiful.

Aristolochia durior (macrophylla, sipho) One of the plants that botanists are frequently renaming, this is the most frequently seen of the genus, although the reasons for this are not obvious. It is a vigorous deciduous climber that will reach a height of 30 ft and will spread widely in all directions. It is really grown as a foliage plant and is useful for clothing unsightly outhouses in the summer. The leaves are heart-shaped and can be very large, up to 10 in. long and 7 in. across. They are slightly downy on the underside. The flowers are small, only about 1½ in. long and are yellowish green on the outside but the inside of the mouth is purple. When the plant is established these flowers are produced in some profusion, but as a general rule they are hidden underneath the large leaves, so that they have to be looked for. June and early July is the time to do this.

Aristolochia sempervirens An evergreen species from the Eastern Mediterranean, which is a slow grower and will either grow prostrate or twine up any small obstacle it may meet. It is by no means vigorous. The small leaves are heart-shaped and a shining green, while the flowers are purple, but otherwise resemble those of *A. altissima*. This is a plant for a sheltered position and would probably be unsuitable in the north. Although evergreen, the stems are not very long lived, being replaced by fresh growths from the rootstock.

Aristolochia tomentosa A deciduous climber from the N.E. United States, less vigorous than *A. durior*, but capable of attaining a height of 25 ft. The young stems, the underside of the leaves and even the flower-stems are covered with a grey-white wool.

The leaves are nearly circular, up to 8 in. long and 7 in. across. The flowers resemble those of *A. durior*, except that the orifice is distincly three-lobed. I consider this preferable to its glabrous compatriot, as the woolly growths and undersides of the leaves give it an interest lacking in the more vigorous *A. durior*.

In 1904 E. H. Wilson brought from China and Messrs Veitch introduced to cultivation *A. heterophylla*. This was a more restrained plant, not exceeding 15 ft in height, with quite small ovate leaves, about 3 in. long and flowers that were not only larger than those of the other hardy species, but also more conspicuous with a yellow tube and a purple spreading mouth. W. J. Bean described the flowers as 'pretty and striking'. Unfortunately the plant does not appear to be in commerce, but it is not unlikely that plants still exist in gardens and it might be possible for it to be re-introduced. The other hardy species brought by Wilson from China, *A. moupinensis*, although less showy than *A. heterophylla*, still sounds more interesting than the two N.American species; and it appears curious that it is the least interesting of the hardy species that have remained in cultivation.

BERCHEMIA

The R.H.S. Dictionary says rather severely of these plants: 'The flowers are without beauty and the fruits so rarely produced in quantity as to make these climbers of little worth. They need a good moist loam'. This harsh assessment seems perfectly justified. However, three species are in commerce and they merit a brief description.

Berchemia giraldiana This, like all the genus, is a deciduous climber. It is a vigorous grower and makes several feet of growth in a season. It may ultimately reach a height of 20 ft. The young shoots turn a reddish-brown colour which is not unattractive. The leaves are an oblong-oval in shape and about 2 in. long. The nearly invisible flowers are white, while the fruits are red to start with, eventually turning black. This is probably the best of an indifferent lot.

Berchemia lineata Growing from 10 to 20 ft, this has rather small oval leaves with the veins conspicuously marked on the underside. The small flowers are produced in terminal panicles and are greenish-white in colour. The fruit is blue-black, about the same size as Elderberries.

Berchemia racemosa This does not climb with much enthusiasm, although the stems do twine and it is best regarded as a sprawling shrub, needing support. The leaves are oval with a heart-shaped base, up to 3 in. long and 1½ in. wide. The flowers are in quite large terminal racemes. W. J. Bean says that it is a striking plant when well furnished with its fruits, which pass from red to black, but that they are so rarely borne in our climate, that it is not useful enough. At one time there was a variegated form of this plant available, with creamy marks on the leaves. This appears to have been lost.

BILLARDIERA

There is only one species that is hardy enough to be grown outside in this country and that needs a sheltered position and is usually grown in only the south and west. This is **Billardiera longiflora.** It is a slender, evergreen climber which is not likely to exceed 5 ft in height. In July it carries ivory-coloured, tubular flowers that are about an inch in length. These are produced from the upper leaf-axils singly. They are followed in October by dark blue berries of about the same size as the flowers. These are said to be edible and not disagreeable. There is also a form with white berries, but the blue-fruited form is more popular. Since they are small plants, it should be possible to grow the two forms together, so that both blue and white berries were produced at the same time. The plant is not a rapid grower, although it will start to flower when only a foot high. It needs wall protection and a fair amount of sunshine. I have seen it growing quite happily against a south wall without any shading at the root, but it is certainly better if this can be applied in some way. It grows slightly more enthusiastically in acid soil, but will also thrive where it is slightly alkaline. They like a loamy root run, so are not likely to be happy in shallow chalky districts. However since they have not a very extensive root system, it is always possible to excavate a hole a yard square and 18 in. deep and fill this with a suitable mixture.

CELASTRUS

There are a large number of Celastrus known, but only four species seem to be in cultivation. Some of the species are unisexual, and, since their main attraction is their fruits, it is necessary in this case to obtain plants of each sex. Even those species with hermaphrodite flowers seem to fruit better if there is a possibility of cross fertilisation. They are all vigorous climbers, usually reaching to 20 ft and in some cases spreading as well, so that they are at their best when enabled to climb up trees or very large shrubs.

The more vigorous species will not do the tree much good and one that is not otherwise much prized should be selected as a host. The flowers are small and usually greenish white, but the fruits are very brilliant when ripe. They resemble peas until they are mature, when they split open to reveal a coloured inner surface, while the seeds are surrounded by a brilliantly coloured fleshy aril. The fruits are produced in great quantities and remain on the trees for some time, as birds do not go for these with much enthusiasm. Celastrus are thus conspicuous in the early winter, when the garden is usually at its least interesting. It is a good idea, therefore, to place them, if possible, where they can be seen from the house. They are greedy plants and need a long, cool, loamy root run. They prefer acid soil, but will grow in most soils, although dry chalky soils will need some manuring to encourage growth.

Celastrus angulatus This is probably the most vigorous species in cultivation and since it is also unisexual, which means that at least two plants must be grown, it is not suitable for small gardens. It does not climb so high, but spreads to 20 or 30 ft. It has large leaves, nearly circular, up to 8 in. long and 6 in. across. The small greenish flowers are in terminal panicles up to 6 in. long and are followed by fruits which have an orange interior against which the red seeds stand out conspicuously.

Celastrus hypoleucus (hypoglaucus) This usually has hermaphrodite flowers and one plant should produce seeds. This is a fairly vigorous climber with the young shoots covered with a pink waxy bloom, which makes them attractive in themselves. The leaves are oblong-oval in shape, up to 6 in. long and 2½ in. across at their widest; they are pointed, dark green on the upper surface, but a delightful glaucous blue on the underside. It is advisable, therefore, to place it where this glaucous underside of the leaves can be enjoyed. If there is an arch in the garden, it is very suitable for such a structure. Otherwise, if trained up a tree, it will grow out along the branches, but the leaves may be hidden by the tree's own leaves. It is, of course, admirable for a dead tree, if your garden should contain anything so unpleasant. The flowers are produced from the upper leaf axils and in a large terminal raceme that may be 8 in. long. This becomes very handsome when the green pea-like seeds split to show the yellow interior against which the red seeds glow. The next species is probably the best for most gardens, but this one is an admirable second choice.

Celastrus orbiculatus (articulatus) A very vigorous climber which can reach up to 40 ft. It is generally hermaphrodite, but unisexual plants do occur, so it is as well to get a guarantee from your nurseryman that your plant is hermaphrodite. The leaves are variable in shape, usually obovate, but sometimes nearly circular and are a dark green. They may reach a length of 5 in. but this is unusually large. The young growths are armed with spines, but these eventually disappear. The flowers are in short racemes from the leaf axils and are followed by the usual green pea-shaped seeds, which split into three to reveal their gold interior and scarlet seeds. A well-fruited specimen of this is one of the most spectacular of plants in the late autumn and the seeds frequently remain in beauty through to the end of January. This is generally regarded as the most satisfactory species. All of these climbers are at their best after their leaves have fallen.

Celastrus rosthornianus This is only moderately vigorous, reaching a height of 20 ft and having very slender stems. This is also meant to bear bisexual flowers, but occasionally all these nominally bisexual plants may produce unisexual specimens. Of course if the plants are vegetatively propagated (which is done most simply by layering) there is no trouble, but seedlings may be unfortunate. This species has rather thick shining green leaves, which are not very large. The axillary racemes are few-flowered. The fruits show orange-yellow interiors with red seeds. This is not so attractive as the two previously described species, but it is quite handsome when in leaf and its slender proportions make it valuable.

CLEMATOCLETHRA

This genus, which is related to Actinidia, is nearly confined to China in the wild. It is not a very striking genus, although the small white flowers may be produced in some numbers, so that the effect is better than the description might suggest. Their introduction, which took place in the early years of this century, is almost entirely the work of E. H. Wilson, who describes them as growing up forest trees.

Clematoclethra integrifolia This is a moderately vigorous climber, capable of reaching up to 25 ft. The small leaves are ovate or oblong-ovate and the flowers, which are thought to resemble those of *Clethra*, are produced singly, or in groups of three, on slender pedicels from all the upper leaf axils. They are followed by small black berry-like fruits, which are of little interest. It flowers, like the next species, in July.

Clematoclethra lasioclada This will not exceed 15 ft usually and has the young shoots covered with down. The leaves are larger than in the last species, up to 4 in. long and the flowers are produced in few-flowered clusters.

In spite of their intriguing name, suggesting a combination of Clethra and Clematis, this genus is not very decorative.

COCCULUS

At one time two species of Cocculus were in cultivation, but the unisexual *C. carolinus* appears to have been lost and the only remaining climbing species is **C. trilobus.** The small flowers are unisexual, but both sexes appear on the same plant, so that the currant-like fruits are generally formed. The plant is a fairly vigorous deciduous climber and has very attractive foliage. The leaves are roughly heart-shaped, up to 4 in. long and with very marked veins. These give the leaves a characteristically netted appearance, which is by no means unattractive. The inconspicuous flowers expand in August and are followed by racemes of black berries with a blue bloom, which ripen in October. *C. carolinus* has red berries. The plants grow in any reasonable soil and are perfectly hardy. They are propogated by means of root cuttings. Cocculus belongs to the *Menispermaceae*, the Moon-Seed Family, so named because the seeds are shaped like a crescent moon.

HOLBOELLIA

Two species of evergreen twiners are to be found in this genus, which can be grown outside, although one is not reliably hardy. They belong, like *Akebia*, to the *Lardizabalaceae*, but the flowers and fruits are smaller. On the other hand the flowers are very fragrant and can scent the air for some distance around in April, when they unfurl. Although small, they are produced in quite large clusters.

Holboellia coriacea This is a fairly vigorous twining evergreen with a purplish stem. The large leaves are composed of three ovate leaflets that may reach a length of 6 in. and a width of 3 in. They are leathery and a dark glossy green. The small male flowers are purplish in colour and appear in terminal groups, while the greenish-white female flowers appear in the lower leaf axils. The fruits are purple and about 2 in. long. They are a form of pod and contain several rows of black seeds.

Holboellia latifolia This is a tender subject and needs wall protection except in the south-west, and west coast. The compound leaves consist of from 3 to 7 leaflets, which are an oblong oval in shape and up to 5 in. long. The flowers in this species appear in axillary racemes and the colours of the last species are reversed; the male flowers being greenish-white and the females purplish. The fruits are slightly larger, up to 3 in. long and are edible. W. J. Bean said that hand fertilization was desirable, but it would obviously be extremely tedious with a large plant and one would have to rely on natural fertilization.

Both these plants are handsome in their foliage and valuable for their fragrance in early spring.

JASMINUM

We have already had to deal with some jasmines in chapter II and there are two other species that seem to be spreading shrubs rather than climbers. There remain, however, a certain number of bona-fide twiners and it is with these that we are concerned here. They are all very vigorous and can be hard pruned in the winter, if they are becoming too exuberant. An exception to this is the tender *J. polyanthum*, which requires any pruning to be done after flowering is completed in late spring. They are not at all fussy as regards soil and, though they like a cool root run, will thrive in situations where the roots are unshaded.

Jasminum beesianum This, also, is best pruned after flowering. It is a deciduous or semi-evergreen twiner and is distinguished from the other species described here by its simple leaves; those of all the others are compound. These leaves are lance-shaped, opposite and about 2 in. long. The rosy-pink flowers appear in May. They are rather small and are produced in groups of three. They do have the genuine Jasmine fragrance, but a better pink jasmine is the hybrid between this and *J. officinale*, known as *J.* × *stephanense*.

Jasminum officinale This is the most well-known of the jasmines with its heads of fragrant white flowers produced from June onwards. It is very vigorous making several feet of growth in a season. It is basically deciduous, but may keep some of its leaves throughout the winter in mild districts. The leaves are composed of several leaflets arranged opposite each other, with a single terminal leaflet, which is twice the size of the others. Each leaflet is more or less lance shaped. This is the only shrub that I have ever seen causing damage to a building. In this case the pointing between the bricks was rotten and the shoots had penetrated between them, rooting as they went, and doing considerable damage before it was detected, so if you are thinking of growing it against a brick wall, be warned and see that the pointing is in good order, before planting. In any case the plant looks rather better scrambling among trees and shrubs. There are two varieties as well as the type in cultivation. The variety known as *affine* is the one to purchase. This has larger flowers carried in more numbers on each cyme. It is equally fragrant and considerably more decorative. The variegated *aureum* or *aureo-maculatum* has creamy-yellow blotches on the leaves and seems to me, personally, a revolting variation. However we do not all think alike.

Jasminum polyanthum This is easily the best of the jasmines, but unfortunately can only be considered hardy in the mildest districts; even in these a severe frost may kill the over-wintering flower buds. The plant itself will grow in comparatively cold districts, but the results are very frustrating, as the plant makes growth every summer, only to be cut down during the winter. It is magnificent in a cold greenhouse. The habit and leaves are very similar to *J. officinale*, although the plant is more markedly ever-green. The flowers, which are produced in the greatest profusion, are white with a pink flush on the exterior and very fragrant. Out of doors it may be expected to flower in late April and early May; in the greenhouse it flowers earlier. If it is not checked the plant is very vigorous. It can be propagated easily from cuttings, which will reach flowering size in fifteen months. The buds appear in the leaf axils in autumn and will only tolerate a very few degrees of frost. I wonder that no one has tried to cross this with *J. officinale* in the hopes of obtaining the hardiness of the one with the intense floriferousness of the other. Possibly it has been tried and there is some hybridity bar.

Jasminum pubigerum There are quite a number of summer flowering Jasmines, with flowers similar to those of *J. officinale* in shape, but yellow in colour. Most of these, such as *J. farreri*, the rather tender *J. floridum* and *J. revolutum* are straggling shrubs, although they can be trained against walls. The only genuine climber is *J. pubigerum*. This is an evergreen twiner with glossy pinnate leaves, similar in shape to those of *J. officinale* and clusters of rather small yellow flowers in late summer and autumn. It may be damaged in severe winters, but since it flowers on the current year's growth, this is not of any very great importance. It should certainly be put in a reasonably sheltered spot and wall protection is probably advisable. From the point of view of flower display the allied, but shrubby, *J. revolutum* is preferable.

Jasminum × stephanense As already mentioned, this plant is the result of pollinating *J. beesianum* with *J. officinale*. The cross has resulted in a vigorous climber with leaves that may be entire or pinnate and clusters of flowers that are pale pink and fragrant. These appear in mid-summer and, for some reason, are not quite so attractive as the description suggests. Possibly it is because they are produced over a space of six weeks, but seldom in very great quantity. The hybrid is certainly an improvement on *J. beesianum* itself and I may have been unfortunate in the plants that I have seen.

All the jasmines are easily propagated by cuttings of half-ripe wood and seem indifferent to soil, although I suspect that *J. pubigerum* might not relish too much lime.

KADSURA

The only species in cultivation is **Kadsura japonica.** This belongs to the Magnolia family, but the flowers are small and inconspicuous. They are also unisexual, and though in theory flowers of both sexes are borne on the same plant, this cannot be relied upon. Since the main attraction of the plant is in its heads of red berries, this is a serious matter. The plant is evergreen, with slender pointed lanceolate leaves, up to 4 in. long and 1½ in. across. The flowers, which are cream-coloured are borne singly on slender pedicels from the leaf axils of the current year's growth. The plant will not exceed 10 ft in growth and needs wall protection. There is a variegated form, in which the leaves have a creamy-white margin. The clusters of red berries are the most attractive feature of the plant, but it does sound as though at least two plants are necessary for these to be obtained.

17 *Actinidia kolomikta*

18 *Lathyrus latifolius*

19 *Pharbitis tricolor*

20 *Cobaea scandens*

21 *Polygonum baldschuanicum*

22 *Celastrus orbiculatus*

23 *Tropaeolum speciosum*

24 *Eccremocarpus scaber*

25 *Schizandra rubrifolia*

26 *Solanum jasminoides*

27 Leaves of *Lonicera japonica aureo-reticulata*

28 *Jasminum nudiflorum*

29 *Holboellia coriacea*

30 *Rubus henryi*

31 *Billardiera longiflor*
in flower

32 *Billardiera longiflor*
in fruit

LAPAGERIA

This is one of the most beautiful climbing plants in cultivation, but it must be admitted that its successful culture is by no means easy. However there are some points about which there seems to be general agreement. It requires acid soil that is fairly light and well enriched with leaf mould or peat; a cool shady situation and it must not be allowed to dry out in the summer. The plant is a native of Chile and a member of the Lily family.

It has rather thin twisting stems, which lengthen to about 12 ft. They have elongated heart-shaped, evergreen, rather leathery leaves and pendulous, bell-shaped crimson flowers about 3 in. long and 2 in. across, which are produced from July onwards. When the plant is well established, it will produce fresh shoots from the rootstock each year. The plant will tolerate a certain amount of frost, but not too much, so that in cold districts it needs a sheltered position, such as a north-west facing wall. It is generally agreed that the best way to obtain good plants is to raise them from seed, but since they usually appear to be unattainable, this is a counsel of perfection. Failing seeds, it is best to get a plant from a really reliable nursery, as it has been found that unsatisfactory plants never thrive. Plants can be propagated by means of layers, but this is not always satisfactory out of doors and is better done in gentle heat. Seed seems to give the best results if sown as soon as ripe. The plant dislikes root disturbance.

Although in most parts of the country the plant requires wall protection, the flowers are better displayed if the plant can be trained over some arching, whence the dangling bells will show off to more advantage. I appear to have omitted to state that this is a monotypic genus and that the only species is **Lapageria rosea.**

When the young plant is put in, it must be given protection against slugs and this must be renewed whenever young shoots are emerging. Slugs seem to be unable to walk over zinc, so it is quite simple to surroung the plant with a circle of perforated zinc, which can be obtained from most builders' merchants. If you obtain a strip about 10 in. wide and bury 5 in. in the ground and let the other 5 in. protrude, this should give ample protection, although it is as well to put down a few pellets, in case you have left some slugs inside the protective ring. The flowering shoots persist for several years, but will eventually die, when there are sufficient replacements. These dead shoots should be carefully cut off at the root and removed. In the greenhouse aphids are frequently a destructive pest on the young shoots, and, though they appear to be less troublesome outside, the young shoots should be frequently examined and sprayed immediately any infection is observed. There used to be a white-flowered form which was particularly prized, but it seems to have been nearly lost to cultivation in this country and is certainly not in commerce at the moment.

LARDIZABALA

The only one of the two species grown is **L. biternata.** This is a fairly vigorous evergreen climber with its leaves in threes; they may consist of 3, 6, or 9 leaflets and the central leaflet in each group of three is the largest. They are roughly oval in shape and range from 2 to 4 in. long. The plant is dioecious. The male plants are the most conspicuous in flower. The flowers are produced in racemes drooping from the leaf axils and about 4 in. long. The actual flowers are small and white, but they are enclosed in large purple fleshy sepals, so that the effect is of a spike of purple and white flowers. The female flowers are similar and slightly larger, but they are only produced singly on a slender stalk from the leaf axils. On the other hand it has sausage-shaped fruits about 2 in. or 3 in. long, which are edible.

This is an attractive plant, but it is very tender and seems to be confined to Hampshire and counties to the west and those other parts of the west coast, which receive a mild climate from the Gulf Stream. It is a Chilean plant and requires the special conditions that most plants from that country seem to require; a cool moist root-run in acid soil and a mild equable climate.

LONICERA

The honeysuckles are among the most loved of climbers for their attractive flowers and very often also for their delicious fragrance. There are some quite spectacular plants which have no scent, but are still worth growing for their flowers. When we come to the individual descriptions I shall write fragrant or scentless directly after the plant's name. Most of the species will grow in any soil, but a few of the N.American species do better when the soil is acid. They are mainly fairly vigorous and will ramp up trees and over bushes. Most species are deciduous, but some are evergreen. Nearly all of the climbers have roundish leaves which are placed in opposite pairs at intervals along the stem. These are either stalkless or have very short stems. The flowers are usually produced in terminal panicles and are trumpet-shaped. The genus has been divided into three sections; most of the climbers belong to the section *Periclymenum*, but a few belong to the section *Nintooa*, notably *L. alseuosmoides* and *L. japonica*. These are evergreen and produce their flowers in pairs from the leaf axils and are less ornamental than the plants in the *Periclymenum* section. The other section, *Xylosteum* or *Chamaecerasus* are bushy shrubs and do not climb. The majority of honeysuckles climb to about 20 ft, but some of the *Nintooa* section may well go up to 30 ft in time. They resemble most climbers in liking to have their roots in shade and they will also flower in comparatively shady conditions, although they prefer to climb out into the sun. I have, however, grown them on a north wall and secured quite an amount of flower. If they are to be grown against walls, they require some wire trellis as a support, or they can be grown on another climber or wall shrub. The flowers are followed by berries, which are usually red and in some seasons make a brilliant and unexpected display. Although a few of the most spectacular species are tender, the majority are easily grown and hardy climbers, that will succeed in practically any position.

Lonicera alseuosmoides Fairly fragrant. This is a Chinese evergreen species with rather atypical leaves. They are long and narrow, about 2 in. long, but only about ½ in. across. The shoots are all very slender and, like so many of the plants in this group (*Nintooa*) the plant tends to make a tangle of intertwining stems. The flowers are produced in pairs in the terminal axils, so as to give the effect of quite a sizeable panicle and are produced from July until September or October. The flowers are rather small with a yellow exterior and a purple interior, reversing the usual honeysuckle colour scheme. They are followed by black-purple berries.

Lonicera × americana (italica, grata) Fragrant. This is a strong growing climber which is the result of a hybrid between the hardy, *L. caprifolium* and the more handsome, but slightly tender Mediterranean *L. etrusca*. Why it should have been given the misleading name of *americana* (the culprit was Koch) is rather baffling. This is a really first rate plant, with purplish young shoots, the usual oval leaves in pairs, which may be 3 in. long, and at the end of the shoots the leaves are united in a sort of cup. From this cup the main whorls of flowers emerge; there may be several, one above the other and they are supplemented by additional whorls coming from the upper leaf axils. This may result, in a vigorous specimen, in a panicle of flowers a foot long and 8 in. across. The flowers are normally yellowish, with a purple suffusion, but at one time there were reddish and purple forms known. They do not appear to be in commerce at the moment. Each individual flower is about 2 in. long and 1½ in. across at the trumpet-shaped top. It flowers in late June.

Lonicera × brownii (fuchsioides, plantierensis) Scentless. This deciduous climber is a hybrid between two N. American species, the handsome, but tender *L. sempervirens* and the hardy *L. hirsuta*, which is no longer in cultivation. This is not a vigorous grower, but is floriferous and very striking with its terminal whorls of scarlet, tubular flowers. It is quite hardy and can be grown anywhere, although it might not be happy with a very alkaline soil. The plant usually starts to flower at the end of May and will continue until the end of August, never making a great splash, like some of the others, but being continuously interesting and attractive. Like the other hybrid honeysuckles, it has to be propagated vegetatively. Cuttings of half-ripe shoots will generally root quite easily.

Lonicera caprifolium Fragrant. This, rather vigorous, deciduous, climber is easily distinguished from most others, by the fact that the leaves below the flowers are united to form a sort of saucer. The ivory, pink-tinged flowers are produced at the end of June and the beginning of July and there is also a pure white form. This is a plant that has no objection to limy soils and has been found wild in S.E. England, although these plants are thought to be escapes from cultivation. Some forms flower as early as May. The berries are orange-red and are sometimes showy.

Lonicera ciliosa. Scentless. This is a N. American species and is of only moderate vigour. Like so many of these American plants the flowers are tubular and do not open out into a trumpet. It gets its specific epithet from the leaves being edged with hairs. The flowers are produced in a terminal spike of several whorls in June and are usually yellow with a purple flush. However forms have been recorded with orange-scarlet or purplish flowers so there is always a chance of something good turning up. I have not seen the berries and they are not described in any book of reference to which I have had access.

Lonicera etrusca Scented. A very vigorous, but tender climber, from the Mediterranean. In appearance it is like a very large-flowered and floriferous *L. periclymenum*, the common Woodbine, but it does not seem to give of its best in this climate and is better replaced by the hybrid *L.×americana*. The plant will start to flower in July and continue for some six weeks. The flowers are cream with a purple suffusion outside, and, as the flower ages, it turns a deeper yellow. The young shoots are purplish.

Lonicera giraldii An evergreen member of the *Nintooa* section, but scentless. This is remarkable in that all its parts are covered with yellow hairs, giving the plant a very distinctive appearance. The leaves are a narrow oblong up to 3 in. long, but not more than 1 in. across and usually less. The flowers are produced in small terminal panicles and are a curious shade of reddish-purple which contrast markedly with their very conspicuous yellow stamens. The berries are a blackish-purple. This is quite a striking plant with its yellowish appearance and its general hairiness. It is apparently quite hardy, although I would be doubtful whether it would thrive in really cold districts. It flowers in early July or late June.

Lonicera glaucescens Scentless. A deciduous N.American species with yellow tubular flowers and agreeable leaves with a blue-green underside. It flowers in June and July. Apart from its attractive leaves, this is not so ornamental as some of the other N. American species. Probably it requires acid or neutral soil.

Lonicera×heckrottii Fragrant. A hybrid between the tender N. American *L. sempervirens* and a European species, thought by Rehder to be *L.×americana*. This has brought fragrance to the brilliant colour of *L. sempervirens*. On the other hand it has practically inhibited its climbing capacity and *L.×heckrottii* is rather a spreading shrub than a true twiner and will probably need some artificial support. The flowers, which are more or less tubular are about 1½ in. long and are orange-yellow with a purple-crimson exterior. The plant is perfectly hardy and, apart from its rather debile habit, remarkably satisfactory. The leaves are glaucous on the underside and are joined together below the flower buds, in a manner suggestive of either *L. caprifolium* or *L.×americana*. The plant starts to flower in June and continues until August.

Lonicera henryi Scentless. A very vigorous evergreen climber, which is useful for making a permanent screen. It will reach a height of 30 ft and make a dense thicket, like so many of the *Nintooa* section. Again the leaves are rather atypical, being up to 4 in. long and only 1 in. across. The young shoots are covered with down, which disappears as they age. The reddish-purple flowers appear in June in rather small terminal clusters and are followed by blackish fruits. This is not one of the most ornamental honeysuckles, but it can be very useful, as its leaves make an elegant screen to any unsightly object.

Lonicera hildebrandiana Fragrant. I mention this because it is listed by some nurserymen, but, in spite of its mouth-watering description, it is really a plant for a very large cool greenhouse. Plants do survive from time to time in places like the Isle of Wight and Cornwall, but even here a really bad winter may cause considerable damage. The plant is a native of Burma and Siam, as well as China, and so, even though it is found high up, it can scarcely be expected to like even our mildest parts. The plant is evergreen and very vigorous, growing 60 to 80 ft in the wild. It is the largest of all honeysuckles with leaves up to 6 in. long and 4 in. across, while each flower is 6 in. long and 4 in. across, so that a whole inflorescence is breathtaking. If tried out of doors, it needs a very warm wall to produce flowers; without this it will grow vigorously, but abstain from flowering. It is really a plant for Mediterranean gardens, as it is too large to grow in most greenhouses and only possible out of doors in a very few localities.

Lonicera implexa Slightly fragrant. This is a rather tender, evergreen, Mediterranean honeysuckle, rarely more than 8 ft high and it seems to do best on a west wall. The leaves are the usual ovate shape, about 2 in. long and pleasantly glaucous on the underside. The upper leaves join to form a sort of cup in which the stalkless flowers rest. These flowers, which will emerge from June until August, are about 2 in. long. The outside is yellow, suffused with pink, while the inside is white which ages to yellow. This should be borne in mind when thinking of a not too vigorous climber for a west wall.

Lonicera japonica Very fragrant. This is a vigorous evergreen twiner capable of reaching 30 ft, and branching frequently to make a dense mass. If it is being grown to form a screen, it requires pruning each winter, as otherwise the lower portions are apt to become bare. The young stems are downy and the stems are consistently hairy, although this is not very apparent. The flowers are produced in pairs from the upper leaf axils and appear from June onwards. Below the flowers are a pair of bracts, similar in shape to the round leaves, though much smaller. These bracts serve to distinguish this honeysuckle from the others of the *Nintooa* section in cultivation. Although the flowers are produced over a long period, they never make a very extensive display and, from this point of view, are inferior to many others, but their fragrance is outstanding. The flowers are normally white, aging to yellow, but the variety *flexuosa* (*repens*) has the exterior of the flowers flushed with red, as well as having the young shoots purple in colour and the main veins of the mature leaves are purplish. The form which approximates most closely to the original description of the plant is known as var. *halliana*. There is an attractive variegated form, var. *aureo-reticulata*, in which all the veins and the midrib are bright yellow, which gives the leaf a netted appearance. This variety is very shy flowering. The plant will grow in any soil and is normally perfectly hardy. In exceptional winters it has been killed to the ground, but has always broken afresh. The variegated form seems invariably to lose some of its young growth over winter, but sufficient is retained to keep the plant looking well. The fruit, which is rarely seen, is a black berry.

Lonicera periclymenum Very fragrant. This is the Woodbine of our hedges and woods, with cream and red flowers in whorls. It is a vigorous climber, usually not exceeding 20 ft, but quite capable of going further if necessary. It is quite indifferent to the type of soil in which it grows, but far prefers having its roots shaded. In the wild it usually flowers in July, but there are selected forms, which flower earlier and later. These are var. *belgica*, known as the Early Dutch Honeysuckle, which will flower at the end of May or in early June and which has deep purple flowers and var. *serotina*, the Late Dutch Honeysuckle, which flowers in August and September and again has reddish flowers. If there is room to grow the type and the two varieties, one can have an unbroken display from late May until September. The translucent red berries are sometimes numerous and give an unexpected bonus. One does not usually think of honeysuckles as berrying climbers, but I have often been surprised at the brilliance of the display.

Lonicera similis delavayi (L. delavayi) Fragrant. This is an evergreen climber of the *Nintooa* section, with comparatively large leaves, up to 5 in. long and 2 in. across; ovate-lanceolate in shape and with the underside covered in white down. The flowers are produced in axillary pairs and in a terminal raceme and are yellow with a very slender tube and markedly bent-back lips. They appear in August and are followed by black berries. This is probably the most decorative of the *Nintooa* section in cultivation, although they are never quite so attractive as the best of the *Periclymenum*.

Lonicera splendida Fragrant. This is a very mysterious plant, which only makes spasmodic appearances in cultivation. It is a native of southern Spain, but is found in subalpine regions and so must be able to withstand quite considerable frost. W. J. Bean records that it was sent to Kew by nurserymen from Aberdeen, where it grew very vigorously, making as much as 6 ft of growth in a season, and appeared perfectly hardy. Nevertheless it is only rarely established in gardens. It evidently needs some special conditions and from its habitat one would think that it might be a very hot dry summer. It is a spectacularly attractive plant and is worth every trouble to establish. Good drainage must be a *sine qua non* and it is probably happier in an alkaline soil.

The plant is a vigorous evergreen with glaucous blue-green leaves which are about 2 in. long and nearly as wide. The uppermost pair are united. The flowers have a yellow tube and a reddish trumpet and are borne in a large cluster of thickly packed whorls. They are about the same size as those of the wild Woodbine. I feel that East Anglia and other eastern districts might be the parts of Great Britain most suited to this splendid climber, but no one really knows and it is worth anyone's while to have a go.

Lonicera tragophylla. Scentless. This is one of the most brilliant of all the Honeysuckles and it is a pity that its brilliance has made it unnecessary to have fragrance as well to attract pollinators. This is a vigorous deciduous climber with rather dark glaucous leaves and yellow flowers with a tube that may be 3 in. long and the trumpet may be 1½ in. across. The berries are red. This is a species that only thrives when given a cool root run and a shady position. It will grow and flower in complete shade, but it is more decorative, when it is able to climb through into the sunlight to display its flowers. However, most of the plant should always be in shade. The leaves are as much as 4½ in. long, shortly stalked at the lower levels, but united below the flowers.

Lonicera × tellmanniana Scentless. This is a hybrid between the last species *L. tragophylla* and the handsome, tender *L. sempervirens*. The plants are natives respectively of China and the U.S.A. This is a vigorous deciduous climber with 2 in. long yellow flowers, which are red at the tips and appear a brilliant red in bud before the flowers actually unfurl. The flowers are not in quite such large clusters as those of *L. tragophylla* and are very slightly smaller, but the red colour in the buds and flowers helps to give an equally brilliant effect. This hybrid needs the same conditions as *L. tragophylla* itself and is thus very useful for shady places or north facing walls. Both the last species and this hybrid are perfectly hardy anywhere in the British Isles. *L. tragophylla* will reach 20 ft with ease, *L. × tellmanniana* is slightly less vigorous, but still vigorous enough. Both species and hybrid flower in late June and early July.

This concludes the list of the most ornamental honeysuckles. If you live in a very mild district it might be possible to grow *L. sempervirens* itself. This is only semi-evergreen and is scentless, but has flowers that may be scarlet, orange or yellow. The flowers are tubular rather than trumpet shaped, in spite of its name of the Trumpet Honeysuckle and are produced from June until August. Although a very attractive plant, it is best with cool greenhouse treatment and can only be expected to thrive outside on the west coast. It likes a cool shady root-run and prefers the soil to be slightly acid.

MANDEVILLA

Only one species, **Mandevilla suaveolens,** is even notionally hardy and this would need wall protection. Fortunately it grows very easily and rapidly from seed and so can be quickly replaced, although it is, perhaps, more satisfactory in a cool greenhouse. Apart from being given a wall, it will benefit from additional protection in its first two winters and may then be sufficiently established to be able to face further rigours without too much apprehension. Although the plant grows vigorously to start with, it seldom reaches higher than 12 ft out of doors, so that it is quite suitable for south or west walls, which must be regarded as essential for this shrub. The plant comes from the Argentine, so that its popular name of Chilean Jasmine can only be regarded as perverse. The dark green leaves are an elongated heart-shape and about 3 in. long. The fragrant white flowers are produced in racemes of about 6 flowers that emerge from the upper leaf axils. The flowers are funnel-shaped and about 2 in. long, and are usually produced with some freedom throughout the summer. The time at which they start flowering depends on the particular season, but it is generally at the end of June. The plant can be propagated by cuttings, but seed is easily obtainable and germinates well with gentle heat. This is sown as early in the spring as practicable. It is tempting to keep the plants in pots for a year, but they do not really like this and better results are obtained by potting on the seedlings into 3 in. pots and then hardening them off and putting them into their permanent position at the end of June. They like to send their roots down vertically for some distance and they can be encouraged to do this, by loosening the soil for a good depth in the position in which they are to be planted. In the greenhouse Mandevilla seems to have great attraction for Green Fly and, although this is less tiresome outside, a close watch should be made of the tips of the growing shoots and spraying resorted to, as soon as any infection is noticed. The plant belongs to the Periwinkle family, the *Apocynaceae*, and like many of the family, the stems contain a milky latex. The seed vessels are also characteristic of this family, being very elongated. The large white flowers, produced over a long period and extremely fragrant make this a plant worth the trouble that it will entail for the first two years. It has been recorded as growing from areas that one would assume were uncongenial, so, if a sheltered nook can be found, it is well worth trying in most districts.

MUEHLENBECKIA

Two species of this are grown in gardens, although they are not particularly attractive and one is slightly tender. They are rather short twiners and some species are unisexual.

Muehlenbeckia complexa This is a deciduous twiner, reaching from 6 to 10 ft in height and producing a large number of very slender shoots, which are liable to twine together into a tangle. The plant is of some interest for its very variable leaf shapes. They can be oblong, roundish, heart-shaped or fiddle-shaped and sometimes all these different shapes can be seen on the same plant. The small flowers, which are greenish-white in colour and not very conspicuous occur in small spikes from the upper leaf axils and there is usually a terminal spike as well. They appear in autumn and the perianth persists and becomes enlarged to give a shining-white waxy cup which encloses the small nut-like fruits. At this period the plant is attractive. This is a native of the New Zealand mountains and is fairly hardy, but may be cut to the ground in a severe winter, although it will break again from the roots. It is quite unsuitable for walls, but may be trained over uninteresting shrubs or tree stumps. It will succeed in most soils.

Muehlenbeckia varians This is a mysterious plant, which was described in 1852, but which has never been since found in the wild. Moreover Meissner, who described the plant, did not know where it had been found. It forms a shrubby base from which twining shoots emerge each year and ascend for 6 or 8 ft. At the top they bear a panicle of whitish flowers. This panicle may be 4 in. long and the flowers are followed by nuts enclosed in a fleshy white cup. The leaves are placed rather distantly up the stem and have a white sheath at their base. They are only about 1 in. long and more or less fiddle-shaped, with a slender point. After fruiting the stems die away and are replaced by others the following year. The plant is perfectly hardy, but its charm is rather recondite and it is not likely to be very popular.

PAEDERIA

There is only one hardy species, **P. scandens (chinensis)** and, although this is quite attractive, it has rather an unpleasing smell and is not much grown. It is a deciduous climber, capable of reaching 15 ft or a little more, but not particularly rapid growing. The leaves, which are opposite, are ovate-lanceolate, with a slender point and may be 5 in. long. The flowers come in July and August and are in rather slender terminal panicles. The individual flowers are small, ½ in. long and ¼ in. wide and are white with a purple centre. They are produced in some quantity, which gives them more attraction than the description of the single flower suggests and are followed by orange berry-like fruits, each about the size of a red currant. The plant is a scrambler over tall shrubs in the wild and does best in similar situations in the garden. It is not outstanding, but makes a change from the better-known climbers and is to be preferred, for example to the next plant.

PERIPLOCA

Again only one species is commonly cultivated, although occasionally other species are offered. The one most commonly grown is **P. graeca,** known for some reason as the Silk Vine. This is a deciduous and vigorous twiner that can reach to 30 ft. The oval leaves are 3–4 in. long, dark shining green and persisting for long into the winter. The flowers appear in heads on long peduncles. Each flower is about 1 in. across, slightly starry in shape, purple on the inside and greenish on the outside. They have a strong scent, which is thought, in its native Greece, to be unhealthy. The flowers are followed by long thin fruits, hanging in pairs, each about 4 in. long, which give a curious effect. The stems contain a poisonous, milky latex. July and August are the months in which the flowers can be expected, but they are not always produced with great abandon. The plant will always grow vigorously and is completely hardy in spite of its Mediterranean provenance. Why anyone should wish to grow it is somewhat mysterious. The only really attractive part of the plant is the seed-pod. Some people find the scent attractive, but to most people it is repellent.

POLYGONUM

Again we have only one species to consider, **Polygonum baldschuanicum,** a plant whose generic name has recently been changed to *Bilderdykia*. This is sometimes called the Siberian Vine, although it comes from Turkestan. It is one of the most vigorous, deciduous climbers in cultivation, often making 15 ft of growth in a season and can easily reach a height of 40 ft. It is completely hardy, will grow in any soil and, where sufficient room is available, is remarkably satisfactory. The plant has oval leaves with a heart-shaped base, up to 4 in. long and 2 in. across and the flowers are borne in great abundance in terminal and lateral panicles, so that the plant looks smothered in flowers. They are produced from July until October and are white or pale pink in colour, fading to a darker pink as the nutlets form. Moreover the foliage may also colour somewhat in the autumn, so it is evident that we have admirable value for money with this plant. Seed is rarely set, in this country, but the plant is easily propagated by means of cuttings. Although it will grow anywhere, it is at its most exuberant when given a moist deep root-run. Although this is now one of the most widely-grown of climbers, and is possibly not prized as it should be on that account, it is of comparatively recent introduction. The plant was not discovered until 1883 and has only been in gardens since 1894. Although it is naturally very vigorous, it will tolerate hard pruning and so can be kept in bounds. Apart from its roots, it likes to grow with a great deal of light and is not so satisfactory in a very shady position.

There are two other climbing Polygonum, which are occasionally found in lists, although neither are popular. *P. aubertii* is similar to *P. baldschuanicum*, but the flowers are either a pure white or white with a greenish tinge and the flower panicles are rather more slender. The leaves are said by Rehder to be more handsome than those of the more popular plant. *P. multiflorum* is somewhat tender. It has a tuberous root, from which stems from 6 to 15 ft high emerge. The flowers and leaves are not very different from those of *P. baldschuanicum*, but the young stems are bright red in colour, which gives the plant some attraction and its more restrained growth may make it more suitable for restricted situations.

SCHIZANDRA

This is a rather small genus belonging to the Magnolia family. The plants are dioecious and, as in many cases the fruits form the principal ornament, this entails having at least two plants. However one species is well worth growing for its flowers alone. This is the species sometimes called *S. rubrifolia* and sometimes *S. grandiflora rubrifolia*, which is among the most charming of all climbers. All the species like a cool root run, but will grow in any soil. Those who have seen the late Sir Frederick Stern's garden at Highdown will recall how well they flourish on the chalk. They are slow-growing and most will not exceed 20 ft and 15 ft seems nearer the mark. The fruits appear as a spike of red berries, sometimes 4 or 5 in. long, and if sexed plants can be obtained, it is well worth growing two. They can both be grown up the same host. Apart from seeds, propagation seems very difficult. Cuttings do not root at all easily and layering seems the best possibility. All the species in cultivation are deciduous although evergreen species are known.

Schizandra glaucescens A deciduous climber of moderate growth with obovate leaves that have a glaucous underside. The rather small flowers appear on stalks that are about 1 in. long and are orange red in colour. When both sexes are present, the female plant will produce 4 in. spikes of scarlet berries. The flowers appear in late May and early June.

Schizandra propinqua The type is not very hardy and this plant is represented in gardens by the var. *sinensis*, which is found in China, as the name implies. This is one of the most vigorous of the genus and can eventually reach a height of 30 ft. Whereas the other two cultivated species have ovate leaves, those of this variety are oblong lance-shaped. The flowers are produced on very short stalks in the leaf axils and are yellowish in colour. The fruit clusters are scarlet, but the spike is shorter than in the other species.

Schizandra rubrifolia This enchanting plant has quite large pendulous flowers of a glowing ruby-red. It is best planted so that one can look up at the flowers, which emerge with the young leaves and may be out in late April in a favourable year. It is not very vigorous, eventually reaching about 15 ft, but taking several years to do so and it likes rather shady conditions. In my garden it is growing up a medium-sized apple tree and appears very content in this situation. If both sexes are grown, the female plant will produce spikes up to 5 in. long of small red berries. Why this enchanting plant is a rarity in gardens is mysterious. It is certainly available from Hilliers and probably from other nurserymen; it is perfectly hardy and will grow in all soils. Although it may be necessary to wait a short time before the plant establishes itself, it will thereafter give continuous pleasure. The flowers are produced from the leaf axils. Each flower is solitary on its stem, but several are produced from each axil and the plant is covered with flowers when it is at its best. If you are looking out for something that is attractive and 'different', you need look no further.

SENECIO

The vast genus of the groundsels, contains plants of every description from annual weeds to shrubs. Among these are a few climbers, but only one is hardy. This is **Senecio scandens**, an evergreen twiner that can reach up to 15 ft. The leaves are roughly triangular in shape and up to 4 in. long. The individual flowers are not particularly large, but are produced in great numbers in a compound panicle of terminal and axillary clusters. They are bright yellow and make a considerable display. The plant will grow in most soils and is valuable on account of its late flowering. It is rarely in flower before September. Although all British writers assume that it is fully hardy, Rehder in his *Manual of Cultivated Trees and Shrubs* suggests that it is somewhat delicate. It should perhaps be treated with some caution.

SINOFRANCHETIA

This is a monotypic genus of the *Lardizabalaceae*. The only species is **S. chinensis.** The plant is a vigorous deciduous twiner capable of reaching 40 ft. The young branches and the young leaves are covered with an attractive purplish bloom. It has large trifoliate leaves borne on very long stalks, often as long as 9 in. These leaves rather resemble those of a Scarlet Runner Bean in shape and size, but they have an attractive glaucous underside. The white flowers are unisexual and inconspicuous, produced in short hanging racemes. However the fruits are not unattractive, being about the size of a grape and lavender-purple in colour. This is quite a useful climber for tall trees and is completely hardy. There are, undoubtedly, more exciting plants.

SMILAX

This is a genus of the Lily family, allied to Asparagus and characterized by thorny stems, heart-shaped leaves, inconspicuous flowers, but quite showy berries. *S. rotundifolia* is the hardiest and the only one generally available, but two other species were popular in former times and might be re-introduced, so they will be given brief descriptions.

Smilax excelsa This is a very vigorous deciduous climber, that can reach to the top of tall trees. The stems are thorny and ascend first by twining, and then they obtain additional support by means of their thorns. The heart-shaped leaves may reach a length of 5 in., but are usually somewhat less. The main attraction of the plant lies in the clusters of red berries that may be produced in some profusion. The plant is reasonably hardy, but is not suitable for very cold localities.

Smilax hispida A deciduous climber that is capable of reaching 40 or 50 ft and is only suitable for growing on large trees. The leaves are egg-shaped with a heart-shaped base, up to 5 in. long and 3½ in. across. The small flowers are formed in many flowered umbels and are succeeded by dark blue berries, which are conspicuous because of their large numbers. The plant gets the name *hispida* from the bristles that cover the stems. No Smilax is in the front rank of climbers, but this useful where a large subject is required and it has proved to be hardy.

Smilax megalantha An evergreen climber capable of reaching 20 ft and so less vigorous than the other species in this list. The stems are armed with long spines, up to ½ in. and the shoots are greyish in colour. The large leaves, which are one of the plant's main attractions, are broadly ovate and may reach a length of 9 in. and 6 in. across. The berries are an attractive coral red. This sounds as though it were the most attractive of the species that were formerly in cultivation and one would be happy to see it again.

Smilax rotundifolia Known in its native U.S.A. as the Horse Briar, this is a vigorous climber that will reach from 30 to 40 ft. The leaves may be round, as the specific epithet suggests, but are sometimes heart-shaped. The berries are black in colour, but have a glaucous bloom like the Sloe and are produced in clusters of from 3 to 6. In mild districts and warm winters the plant may be partially evergreen. This is the hardiest of all the species.

All the plants produce unisexual flowers and although there are usually both sexes present on the same plant, this cannot be relied upon. Since, with the exception of *S. megalantha*, their main attraction lies in their fruit, they can only be regarded as suitable for gardens that have a certain amount of woodland.

There is also a herbaceous species **S. herbacea**, of which seed is offered by Thompson and Morgan. This throws up yearly twining stems that can reach 10 ft. The flowers, which smell repellent, are borne on long-stalked umbels and are followed by blue-black berries. The rather leathery leaves may be roughly triangular in shape or lance-shaped. The plant is little more than a curiosity and has little garden merit.

SOLANUM

Solanum jasminoides is a much branching twiner that needs wall protection in all districts away from the west coast. The plant is a semi-evergreen, retaining its leaves in mild situations and shedding them where the climate is less equable. The plant will reach a height of about 20 ft, but may well spread to a greater width. The individual flowers are about ¾ in. across, produced in numerous racemes, each raceme bearing about 10 flowers. They are normally a very pale violet in colour, but there is a white form which is even more popular. It usually begins to flower at the end of August and continues through September to the end of October. Some of the leaves are small and entirc, while others are larger and divided like a potato leaf. Selected clones have been given the varietal names of *floribundum* and *grandiflorum*. The plant prefers acid soil. Although it is tender, it can be found against walls in cold districts and is one of the climbers that do not appear to resent being planted against a south wall, without any shading at the root. It is very acceptable for its abundant and late flowers.

STAUNTONIA

Only one species, **S. hexaphylla,** is grown and, away from the west coast, needs wall protection. This is a fairly vigorous evergreen with long stalked leaves composed of a number of leaflets ranging from 3 to 7. Each individual leaflet is a pointed oval about 3 in. long, so that the whole leaf is quite sizeable. This is another member of the *Lardizabalaceae* and has the usual spike of unisexual flowers; the males at the tips and the females nearest the stem. These flowers are small, but fragrant, and appear in April. The fruits are as large as a walnut and purple in colour. They are edible and, apparently, an article of commerce in Japan. The plant is an attractive evergreen climber, but needs pruning when grown against a wall to keep it in bounds. It is scarcely distinguished enough for a house wall, but can clothe other walls or fences in a satisfactory manner.

TRACHELOSPERMUM

A genus of the *Asclepiadaceae* with evergreen leaves, except in one species, and fragrant flowers, which resemble those of Jasmine. They all require wall protection and cannot be expected to thrive in very cold districts. They appear to prefer acid soil and one is advised to incorporate peat with the soil when planting them.

Trachelospermum asiaticum (divaricatum) This is one of the hardier species and might succeed in mild districts without wall protection. It is a fairly vigorous plant that will reach from 15 to 20 ft in height. The narrow leaves are up to 2 in. long, but only ¾ in. wide and are produced in large numbers. The flowers are a pale buff in colour and produced in clusters about 2 in. across. They are very fragrant.

Trachelospermum jasminoides This is the least vigorous of the species in cultivation; it rarely exceeds 12 ft in height, although it is capable of the same dimensions as *T. asiaticum*. The evergreen leaves are an elongated oval, pointed at each end and slightly larger than those of the last species, reaching a length of 3 in and a width of 1 in. The flowers are also slightly larger and a clear white in colour, produced in a compound of terminal and axillary racemes. The plant is extremely fragrant, but is the least hardy of the three in cultivation and is best kept for the milder districts. There is a variegated form, var. *variegatum*, with an ivory edge to the leaves and also a bronze-leaved form, var. *wilsonii*. They are both weaker growers and seem to me to have very little advantage over the typical form. Although the leaves are produced plentifully, they are too small for any variegation to make much effect.

Trachelospermum majus (japonicum) This differs from the other two species in its deciduous habit. It is also far more vigorous, capable of reaching 40 ft or more. The young shoots are downy and the leaves, which are of similar dimensions to those of the last species, often colour well before falling. The white flowers are not large individually and the plant is less fragrant than the other two species. However this does seem to be the hardiest of them all and it is capable of covering a very large area, so it can be recommended where there is a large area of wall to cover. Since it has a good display of flowers and, with luck, a display of autumn colour, it is evidently a valuable plant for the garden. All three species flower in July and August and will grow in any decent soil, although, as already mentioned, they appear to do better when it is slightly acid. If protection is given for the first two winters, both *T. asiaticum* and *T. majus*, will thrive well. They will, in any case, be little affected by frost, but will appreciate the protection, while they establish themselves. *T. jasminoides* should have the same treatment, but is more frost tender and may be flattened by severe winters, although it can then break again from the roots.

TRIPTERYGIUM

These are Asiatic relatives of the Celastrus, but in place of the attractive berries that Celastrus produces, Tripterygium has fruits of a curious winged nature, like those of the Wych Elm. Although the flowers are unisexual, both sexes are found on the one plant, so that fruit is formed fairly regularly. The plants need a shady root run and appear to be tolerant of soil of any reaction.

Tripterygium regelii This is rather a curious plant. If planted in a situation away from other plants, it will form a spreading shrub, that is usually not more than 7 ft in height. On the other hand, if planted among trees or shrubs, it can climb up them to a height of 30 ft. The plant has handsome leaves, which are ovate with a long slender point and may reach a length of 6 in. It is not a particularly rapid grower. The small flowers are produced in large terminal and axillary panicles and the whole inflorescence may be 9 in. long. The flowers are cream-coloured and appear in July and August. They are followed by the curious winged fruits which are greenish-white in colour, but covered to start with by a reddish felt. Unlike the next species, this one is perfectly hardy and is a good tree climber, with its large leaves and quite showy flowers, as well as its curious fruits.

Tripterygium wilfordii The naming of the two species in this genus has led to some confusion. Originally Regel named the last plant *T. wilfordii*, but the younger Hooker had already given that name to the present species. References to *T. wilfordii* previous to 1914, probably refer to *T. regelii*. Anyway the true *wilfordii* is a vigorous deciduous climber, that can reach 40 ft. The inflorescence is large, often a foot long, composed of numerous small white flowers with conspicuous purple anthers. The Wych Elm-like seed heads are reddish-purple in colour. Each seed-vessel is about ¾ in. long and each of the three wings is about ¼ in. wide. Unfortunately the plant is tender and is really only suitable for the west coast. It would grow elsewhere with wall protection, but being so vigorous ,it is not really suitable for most walls. It requires a lot of space and a tree is the obvious host. It could, of course, be tried in sheltered situations in less favoured localities, but the plant will not tolerate much frost. It is a native of Formosa, southern China and Burma, although always at a considerable height. The plant flowers in August and the seeds are formed rapidly afterwards.

WATTAKAKA

Only one species, **Wattakaka sinensis,** is hardy enough to be grown outside, and that will need wall protection in most districts. One feels that it must be worth growing, if only for the sake of writing out its label and telling your friends the name of the plant they are inspecting.

The plant is not very vigorous, rarely exceeding 10 ft in height and has rather attractive heart-shaped leaves, up to 4 in. long and 3 in. across. These are downy on the underside and the young shoots are also covered with down. The flowers are small and white with red dots and are produced in axillary umbels, composed of from 10 to 25 flowers and giving an inflorescence about 3 in. across. They appear over a long period throughout the summer from late June onwards. If seed is set it has the usual attractive shape of the Asclepiads being a pair of long thin follicles, each one about 2 in long. This climber does not seem to mind whether it is growing in acid or in alkaline soil.

The first species to be found was the Indian *W. volubilis*, which was known to the natives of Malabar as wattakaka-rodi and it is from this native name that the genus has its curious spelling.

WISTERIA

After the rather obscure plants that we have had to investigate, it is quite a relief to turn to this popular genus. It is sometimes spelt Wistaria, which indeed it should have been, as Thomas Nuttall named it after Caspar Wistar, a professor of anatomy at the University of Pennsylvania at the end of the 18th century. Unfortunately the name was misprinted, so that Wisteria is botanically the correct spelling.

The species are all fairly vigorous deciduous climbers, which will eventually make quite a thick trunk and so can, with a certain amount of trouble, be trained as standards. If they are being grown against house walls they must be watched with care, as they can get behind rain-water pipes or guttering and are liable to pry them loose. Very few climbers are suitable for growing on tile-hung walls and Wisteria is certainly not among them. Although they like their roots to be in the shade, they only flower well in full sunshine. If, therefore, you wish to grow them against the house, they are best planted on a corner so that their roots will be in a cool place, but so that the plant can be trained round the corner on to a warm wall. They will need fairly rigorous pruning. Ideally all lateral growths, that are not needed to form the framework, should be pruned back to about half their length in the late summer, July and August, and then spurred back to two buds during the winter. A similar treatment should be followed if the plants are being trained over arches or on a pergola. The plants can be trained to ramble through trees or among large shrubs (they look particularly effective in large hollies) and in this case they will soon have to be left to their own devices. Few of us have streams in our gardens over which a bridge is placed, but those who remember the bridge at Wisley will appreciate what a suitable situation this is for a Wisteria, when it is in full flower and its flowers are reflected in the water.

It comes as rather a shock, when one looks into the genus, to find that several species appear to have been in cultivation and disappeared. This applies particularly to two N. American species, which have the advantage of flowering much later than the more popular Asiatic species. I see that Thompson and Morgan offer seed of *W. frutescens*, but the more handsome *W. macrostachya* does not seem to be with us any more. As these American species flower later than the Asiatic ones, their reintroduction would be useful, particularly in cold districts with a history of spring frosts. The plants are all hardy as far as winter frosts are concerned, but the buds start to develop in early spring and are then rather susceptible. Under these circumstances, there is much to be said for the later flowering species, although they are not so handsome as those from China and Japan.

All the species are intolerant of root disturbance and may sulk for a year after being planted. Once they do get away there is no holding them and they will make many feet of growth in a season. They do not flower with much freedom, until they have made a good lot of wood, so patience must be exercised for two or three years, sometimes longer. In recent years there have been reports from all over the country of birds stripping the plants of the flower buds. At the moment there seems to be no really effective protection against this, although enveloping the plant in a substance such as Scaraweb may help. Here again the American species, which bear their flowers at the end of their shoots and so produce their buds later in the season might prove advantageous. Wisterias will grow in any type of soil, although if the soil is shallow a large hole should be excavated to a depth of 18 in. or two feet and then filled with a good soil mixture. Once the Wisteria has filled up this, it will have acquired sufficient strength to maintain itself, although yearly mulches should be indulged in, to prevent the soil becoming utterly impoverished.

Wisteria floribunda (multijuga) This is a plant of Japanese origin, which may reach 30 ft or more. It has large pinnate leaves composed of from 11 to 19 leaflets and each leaf is from 10 in. to 15 in. long. The racemes open from the base downwards, a characteristic that enables one to distinguish it easily from the better-known *W. sinensis*, in which the whole raceme opens simultaneously. The raceme of the type and of the white and pink colour forms is about 10 in. long, but the form usually grown is var. *macrobotrys* (or *multijuga*), in which the racemes are frequently 2 ft long and lengths of 4 ft have been recorded in this country and up to 6 ft in Japan; a fact that sounds incredible, but which appears to be well authenticated. Although these immense racemes are very effective, they are not always produced very plentifully and the plant is slow in coming to flowering size and for most purposes *W. sinensis* is a better plant. The type of *W. floribunda*, which is not common in cultivation, is of a purplish-blue colour (indigo-blue according to Siebold, who first introduced it) but those of var. *macrobotrys* are lavender in colour and with the typical Wisteria honey fragrance. There are forms known with white flowers, a rather poor purplish-pink (var. *rosea*), and with double flowers. At one time there was also a form with variegated leaves, but this was never popular and it is probably not much loss. This usually flowers slightly later than the Chinese Wisteria, about the beginning of June.

Wisteria × formosa This is a hybrid between *W. floribunda alba* and *W. chinensis*. It has the more pinnate leaves of the first species, while the pale violet flowers open simultaneously along the raceme as in the second species. This is in cultivation, but differs little from the species.

Wisteria frutescens A native of the S.E. United States and valuable for its late flowering. At the moment, only seeds are obtainable. This will climb from 30–40 ft and the leaves are composed of from 9 to 15 leaflets. They are from 9 in. to 12 in. long. The racemes are produced on the ends of the current year's shoots, so that the risk of bird damage with this plant would be minimized. There is also no need for summer pruning. The racemes are not very long, not exceeding 6 in. in length, and the shorter racemes are held erect and do not droop. The plant starts flowering in June and continues until August; not making one grand display, like the Asiatic species. The flowers, which are crowded together are a pale lilac-purple, with a yellow spot at the base of the standard. The allied *W. macrostachya* seems to be a better plant, but it would be nice to be able to purchase both.

Wisteria japonica This sounds like another desirable plant that has been temporarily lost to cultivation. This is a plant with a number of slender twining stems and does not usually exceed 20 ft in height. The leaves are from 6 in. to 9 in. long and are composed of from 9 to 13 leaflets. The flowers are produced in July and August in racemes, that may be branched into a panicle, from 6 in. to 12 in. long. They are many-flowered and the individual flowers are only half the size of the more popular species, but they are pale yellow in colour, or sometimes white. This is an unusual plant and should be reintroduced, if only on account of its late flowering and unusual colour. The racemes are produced from the leaf axils of the current year's growth, unlike those of *W. floribunda* and *sinensis*, which come on the second-year wood.

Wisteria macrostachya This is a North American species allied to *W. frutescens*, but a more slender plant with longer racemes. It seldom exceeds 20 ft in height; the leaves are only about 3 in. long, composed of 9 leaflets. The racemes may reach a foot in length and may consist of 90 flowers. They are lilac-purple in colour and appear in June and July. There is no suggestion in any books written at the time that it was in cultivation, that the plant was tender, but it does come from the more southern United States and may prove to be slightly tender. One would like a chance to find out.

Wisteria sinensis The R. H. S. Dictionary says firmly of this plant 'the noblest hardy climber ever introduced' and it would be difficult to contradict this. It can reach an immense size; plants climbing to 100 ft with trunks 5 ft in girth have been recorded and if it can be given a large tree in which it can climb, there are few sights more effective. It will not do the tree any good and may even damage it, but the result is so splendid, that if you have an expendable tree, it is worth doing. Although the leaves are up to 12 in. long, they never consist of more than 11 leaflets a feature which serves to distinguish this from *W. floribunda*, which frequently has many more and never has less. The difference in the flowering has already been remarked. There is a white variety and also one with double flowers, which have quite lost their pea-shape and appear like little rosettes. They are not particularly attractive and the plant is shy-flowering. The type has flowers of a deep lilac-mauve in racemes of from 8 in. to 12 in. and the plant is usually in flower by the end of May. Once it is established the plant is extremely floriferous and with its rich honey-like perfume is one of the glories of any garden, no matter how many choice flowers are grown.

Wisteria venusta For some reason this species, which is not outstandingly attractive, though no Wisteria is ugly, has remained in cultivation, while plants such as *W. macrostachya* and *japonica*, which sound more attractive have been lost. This is quite a vigorous climber, capable of reaching 30 ft. The leaves are from 8 in. to 14 in. long and are composed of 11 leaflets as a general rule. The plant differs from the other species in its persistently downy leaves and young stems. The individual flowers are slightly larger than those of *W. sinensis*, but they are only in short racemes of from 4 in. to 6 in. in length. The form that was given the specific name was introduced from Japanese gardens and has white flowers with a yellow blotch at the base of the standard. There was a also double white form known, though this appears to be no longer available. The wild form with violet flowers has been given the name var. *violacea* and is barely in cultivation. The flowers are fragrant, but much less than those of the larger species. The plant flowers in May and June.

This really concludes the list of shrubby twiners. There may be a few places in the British Isles where it is possible to grow *Araujia sericofera* and *Sollya heterophylla* outside, but they must be very few. The Araujia is not even very attractive; although the white saucer-shaped flowers are fragrant, they are never produced with much abundance. The pollen masses are very sticky and the plant is sometimes called the Cruel Plant, owing to the fact that moths are often caught by the proboscis on these sticky masses. *Sollya heterophylla* is charming, but very frost tender. It has blue flowers over quite an extended period.

II HERBACEOUS TWINERS

There is a motley selection of these, ranging from quite dwarf plants to vigorous climbers. There are a large number of annuals in this list and they generally want sunny positions. Otherwise there is not really very much one can say about these plants as a group and it is probably best to go straight to the individual descriptions.

ACONITUM

Most of the Aconites we know as rather stately plants for the herbaceous bed or border, but there are a few Chinese species that have adapted themselves to twine up low shrubs. All the species mentioned are in cultivation, but it is only *A. volubile* that is easily obtainable and that is generally a matter of purchasing seed.

Aconitum hemsleyanum This is a moderate twiner, usually rising to 5 or 6 ft. The twining stems are herbaceous and arise in the spring from a stout rootstock. The lower leaves are more or less heart-shaped, but the ones higher up the stalk are deeply lobed as is the case with most of the genus. The terminal raceme consists of about 10, rather large, violet flowers of the typical Monkshood shape. These appear in late summer or early autumn. None of these climbing Aconites are particularly showy, but they flower late in the year, when any unusual flower is welcome and they take up little room. They are best planted at the foot of a low shrub and are indifferent as to soil.

Aconitum vilmorinianum From a cluster of thick roots spring the twining stems that will ascend to 6 or 7 ft in the season. The flowers are in lateral, as well as terminal, racemes, which are rather few-flowered. They are a deep bluish-violet in colour. The leaves are deeply 3-lobed and dark green in colour. The plant is valuable for its very late flowering; the first flowers do not appear until September and they continue into October.

Aconitum volubile This is an aggregate species among which are reckoned several plants that have, on occasion, been given specific names of their own. They all resemble each other very closely. This is the most vigorous of the climbing aconites and the very slender stems may twine up to 12 or even 16 ft, which is a lot of growth for a single season. The upper leaves are very deeply lobed into 5 or 7 divisions, those at the base are less divided. The violet flowers are in a lax few-flowered terminal raceme that usually droops somewhat, and are less attractive than those of the other two species.

APIOS

There is going to be a slightly irritating feature of this section, in that I shall be mentioning plants that are not immediately obtainable. I am doing this with some rather desirable plants, in the hope that demand will create a supply. The first of these unobtainable plants is the North American **Apios tuberosa,** known in the U.S.A. as the Ground-Nut.

As the name implies, this is a tuberous perennial. The twining stems will climb from 4 to 8 ft and are furnished with elegantly pinnate leaves, composed of 5–7 small leaflets. The flowers appear in late summer, from August onwards in short, many-flowered axillary racemes. The flowers are chocolate in colour and attractively fragrant; with rather a spicy scent. Another local name is the Cinnamon Vine. The plant was introduced to gardens as long ago as 1640. This is a pleasant little twiner, which would grow in most soils, although I doubt if it would do so well on the chalk. Anyone with friends in the U.S.A. who could send seeds over to them, would have a delightful plant. The small tubers are edible, but must be too fussy to prepare for cooking, even if they were delicious, which there seems no reason to believe.

ASPARAGUS

Most of the climbing Asparagus, including the popular Asparagus Fern, *A. plumosus*, require greenhouse conditions, but there is one species, **A. verticillatus,** which is hardy and of which seeds can be procured. This is evergreen and will reach from 10 to 15 ft in height. It might almost have been included in the previous section, as the stems become somewhat woody as they age. The stems are fairly slender, about ½ in. diameter and are armed with prickles. Asparagus do not have leaves, as a general rule, but leaf-like processes called phylloclades. In *A. verticillatus* these are thread-like and up to 2 in. long and appear in clusters at intervals along the stem. The effect is quite graceful. The flowers are inconspicuous, but are followed by red berries, which are ornamental. This is quite a useful plant for a rather shady position, but is not excessively ornamental. Canon Ellacombe who had a famous garden near Bristol at the end of the last century maintained that the Smilax, *A. medeoloides*, was perfectly hardy. It grows easily from seed and might well be worth trying outside.

BOMAREA

A genus of half-hardy climbers with flowers very similar to those of alstroemerias, from which they are distinguished mainly by their climbing habits. (They also have a different chromosome count, which means that hybrids between the two genera are probably impossible.) Very occasionally firms such as Thompson and Morgan advertise seeds, generally of *B. multiflora*. The flowers are produced in many flowered umbels at the ends of the twining shoots and in most species appear at the end of the summer. The plants should be treated like alstroemerias; the seedlings potted separately as soon as they are large enough to handle and then planted in a deep loamy soil. They are excellent subjects for a cold greenhouse, but are only possible out of doors along the west coast and with wall protection. As the tuberous roots will eventually descend to a great depth, they should become hardier as the plants become more mature and, provided that the emerging shoots are protected against spring frosts, they might prove hardier than the authorities lead one to expect. The other species that are occasionally obtainable are *B. edulis* and *B. kalbreyeri*. There are also a number of hybrids raised in various Botanic Gardens.

BRODIAEA

This is the only bulbous climber to be mentioned. The plant is a real curiosity and is not, so far as I am aware, obtainable in commerce. The plant is a native of California and is probably as difficult to cultivate as are most Californian bulbs, requiring very sharp drainage and protection from excessive damp. They will usually tolerate some frost, particularly this species which would be underground in the winter. There is only the one climbing species, **B. volubilis.** This has a bulb about the size of a walnut and produces in the spring a rosette of linear leaves, that may reach a foot in length. These lie on the ground. The flowering stem then starts to emerge and may twine up to a height of 12 ft, before it opens its umbel of purplish-pink flowers, which are in a head of from 15 to 30 flowers. If bulbs can be obtained from the U.S.A. they presumably require planting under a fairly tall bush, through which the extraordinary twining flower stem could climb. This is a real vegetable curiosity and I can think of no other plant that behaves in a similar way. It is not outstandingly attractive and the more popular low-growing species such as *ixioides* and *laxa* are better garden plants and are easily obtainable. They do not climb, however, and have no part in this book.

CALONYCTION

This is the first of a number of genera with twining habits and large trumpet shaped flowers, known popularly as Convolvulus or Ipomaea, but spread nowadays over a large number of genera. As the plants are so similar in appearance, I feel it may be easier to consider them all together, rather than letting them come in their proper places in the alphabetic order.

Calonyction aculeatum (Ipomaea bona-nox) Known as the Moonflower, this is a greenhouse perennial, but is treated as a half-hardy annual. Seeds should be sown in heat in March and grown in 3 in. pots until the end of May. They are then planted out, generally against a south or west facing wall. Under these conditions they do not much exceed 5 ft, whereas in the greenhouse they will reach double this height. The leaves are generally heart-shaped, sometimes shaped like a spear-head and sometimes three-lobed. The fragrant, white flowers, which are salver-shaped and up to 6 in. across are produced in heads, but flower singly. As the plant is pollinated by night-flying moths, they open at sundown and have faded by the next day. They are useful for floral decorations or planted against the house, in a position where their fragrance can be enjoyed. A pink form of this has been found and, apparently, comes true from seed.

Calystegia is the genus that includes that fearful weed Bell-bine, and all the species, with the exception of the New Zealand **C. tuguriorum,** are liable to ramp around the garden with the same freedom and must be treated with respect. Indeed they are now seldom found in gardens and I know nowhere where they are offered for sale. At one time **C. japonica (pubescens)** was a popular garden plant. This would grow up to 20 ft and had quite large pink flowers; there was also a double variety, which had the advantage of being sterile. Although they were nearly impossible to remove, once they had established themselves, they were extremely showy and effective, flowering as they did from late June until the frosts. I have never seen the controllable *C. tuguriorum*, but it is described as having red-veined, ovate leaves with a slender point and a cordate base, and white flowers, with a greenish throat. The white portions are quite deeply lobed and the plant sounds as though it might well look rather distinguished. The other species which was popular at one time was **C. dahurica** with rosy-purple flowers. None of these seem to be available in commerce, but they probably survive in many gardens.

The majority of **Convolvulus** species in cultivation are not climbers as a general rule, although they may well do some climbing if they meet with obstacles. For example the execrable Bindweed (*C. arvensis*) usually spreads along the ground, but if it meets any obstacle it will start twining up it. Probably the same thing would happen with the attractive purple-flowered *C. althaeoides*, which is usually regarded as a trailer. As matters stand at the moment there are only two twiners in general cultivation, although it is always possible that others may be introduced. The other species are either sub-shrubs or dwarf annuals.

Convolvulus mauritanicus This is a tender perennial, which will, however, flower the first year from seed and can be treated as a half-hardy annual. The seeds are started in heat in March or April, potted into 3 in. pots when large enough to handle and planted out at the end of May when any risk of late frosts should be over. The plant spreads and branches in many directions; the branches will twine together and will also climb up any small shrub that they may meet. Not that shrubs are necessary, they can be trained up the spikes of herbaceous plants. In any case they will not climb very high and the plant is suitable for rock work. The flowers are about 1 in. across and are a good blue colour with a white throat. The first year the plant will start flowering in July, but if it survives the winter, it will flower earlier the second year. In its native haunts of Southern Spain and North Africa it is evergreen. It will not tolerate more than a few degrees of frost. It needs a sunny situation and well-drained soil. It is possible to lift the plants and overwinter them under cover, but they grow so easily from seed, that it may not be worth the trouble.

Convolvulus tenuissimus (elegantissimus) This is a delightful perennial with silvery leaves. The lower leaves are heart-shaped, while the upper ones are cut into numerous linear lobes. From the upper leaf axils the bright rose-pink flowers are produced from June onwards. The plant is very similar to *C. althaeoides*, from which it can be distinguished by its twining stems and its pink, not purple flowers. The plant is a native of the Eastern Mediterranean and should be given stony soil and a sunny position. Normally the stems die down every year, but they may persist through a mild winter. This is not a tall climber, but likes rambling over dwarf shrubs and is an excellent plant for the rock-garden, with its long flowering season, its silvery leaves and its rosy flowers. It is a plant best purchased in the spring, as there is otherwise a risk of losing it during its first winter, before the roots have been able to descend sufficiently deeply to be able to ignore even the hardest frost. Once these roots are well and truly down, the crown of the plant seems to be able to withstand any low temperatures, but before this has happened, plants may be lost during the winter.

It is really rather ironical that at the moment no species of **Ipomaea** as defined by botanists, is in cultivation among the hardy climbers and most of the species that are listed in many catalogues as Ipomaea, must be found under **Pharbitis.** These are all somewhat tender plants and, with one exception, are half-hardy annuals.

Pharbitis × imperialis These Japanese Morning Glories are probably the result of hybridising *P. hederacea* with *P. tricolor.* They require to be raised in heat and it is desirable that this heat should remain fairly constant. They are hardened off and planted out when there is no further risk of frost. Germination may sometimes be hastened by putting the seeds in boiling water and letting this cool with the seeds soaking. The plants usually have heart-shaped leaves, but occasionally they are three-lobed. The flowers are of many colours, with blue tending to predominate.

Pharbitis learii The only perennial in the group. This is, in the greenhouse, a shrubby, evergreen, very vigorous twiner, but it will survive out of doors, although it is cut to the ground every winter and so behaves like an herbaceous plant. It requires a fairly deep soil and the warmest available position.

The twining stems are furnished with trilobed, rather bristly leaves about 4 in. across. The flowers are produced in axillary panicles and in the open air rarely appear before August, although under glass the plant is almost continuously in flower from June onwards. The flowers emerge singly and are an intensely bright blue when they first open. As the day advances they turn a reddish-purple and have closed by the evening, to be replaced the next day by another flower. Although we cannot expect outside the sheets of blue that the plant will produce under cover, it is still a very handsome twiner. The flowers are some 3 in. across. For outside work, plants should be purchased in the spring and not planted outside until June. They should be given every encouragement to make plenty of growth during this first season, by giving them plenty of peaty loam among the roots and some cow or horse manure if possible. They will tolerate a few degrees of frost for a short period and do very well in the south of France, where frost, although rarely prolonged, is not unusual.

Pharbitis purpurea (Convolvulus major) Half hardy annual, but one which can be sown outside at about the same time as you would sow Runner Beans. It may gain a bit, by being raised under heat to start with, but this is not essential. This well-known twiner can reach as high as 10 ft, but from 6–7 seems more usual. The convolvulus-like flowers are usually some shade of purple, but a red form, described rather optimistically as scarlet, white and blue forms are known and there is now a strain with a large percentage of double flowers. Both this species and *P.*×*imperialis* tend to be listed by some seedsmen under the general heading of Ipomaea and one does not always know what one is purchasing. However whatever it may be, the result is usually pleasant enough. All these *Pharbitis* spp have flowers that only last for about 12 hours and sometimes even less, as their popular name of Morning Glory would suggest.

Pharbitis tricolor (Ipomaea rubro-coerulea) This is one of the most popular of half-hardy annuals. It requires to be started in gentle heat, around 55°F, and this should fluctuate as little as possible. Violent fluctuations of temperature appear to cause chlorosis in the young plants. The leaves turn an unhealthy yellow and, although the plant will usually recover, its progress is seriously delayed; some plants indeed will die. No one is quite certain of the cause of this complaint, but uneven temperatures seem to bring it on without fail. The young plants are hardened off in mid-May and planted out as soon as there is no further risk of frost. They will only send up a single twining stem, like the last species, and can happily be grown up a long cane if no other support is available. They require as warm and sunny position as you can find. From 6 to 7 ft is the usual height that they attain. The large flowers are a very intense blue and well-flowered plants are one of the most delightful of climbers from July until September. Occasionally one can find a pale Cambridge Blue cultivar, which is also very attractive and seems slightly more floriferous. All these half-hardy Pharbitis will do better in a hot season, but they must be kept reasonably moist at the root. Too rich a soil may induce too much growth at the expense of flower production, so if you have a rich soil, you must hope for a prolonged autumn.

The last of the Convolvulus family to be considered has the curious name of **Quamoclit**. These are half-hardy annuals with dissected leaves and rather small scarlet flowers, which are produced in some abundance. The flowers survive for rather longer than the more popular Morning Glories, and will probably still be present by the evening.

Quamoclit lobata (Mina lobata) A fairly vigorous half-hardy annual, best started in gentle heat in April and planted out at the beginning of June. The bright crimson flowers are not very large and have an inflated tube. The leaves are markedly three-lobed and the plant may reach anything from 7 to 10 ft. It will start flowering in July and continue until frost puts an end to its life. It requires the same warm situation that the Morning Glories need. In the south the seeds can be planted outside in mid-May.

Quamoclit pennata A slender and not very vigorous climber with pinnate leaves composed of a number of thread-like leaflets. Because of these fine leaflets it acquired in America the name of the Cypress Vine. This has got turned, in this country, into Cyprus Vine, although the plant comes from Central America and has no connection with Cyprus. This does require starting in heat and will not thrive if the summer is cold and wet. If it is warm, the plant covers itself with small, star-shaped, scarlet flowers that have only a very short tube. The plant is an attractive little thing with its feathery leaves and scarlet flowers and may be grown up a spring flowering climber or wall-shrub, without the fear that it will do any damage to its host.

This concludes the enumeration of the climbing members of the Convolvulus family that can be grown out of doors.

CODONOPSIS

It is rather unusual to find climbing plants among the Campanula family, but there are a few, of which Codonopsis is the only hardy genus. The plants come from the Himalaya and West China and are usually found very high up. They are generally tuberous and throw up a number of twining stems every year. They require acid soil which should be well-drained and can easily be raised from seed. There are some non-twining species, which are grown on the rock garden and this is really best for the twining species also, if the rock garden is sufficiently large to carry dwarf shrubs. Two of the species will go to quite a considerable height and can be trained on to large shrubs, but they will be satisfactory on lower ones, as they enjoy rambling about through the shrubs once they have emerged into the light. With the exception of *C. convulvulacea* and *C. vinciflora*, it is desirable, if it is possible in your garden, to plant these on a bank, so that one can see the inside of the bell-like flowers, which are often more interesting than the exterior. Apart from their twining habit, the flowers closely resemble those of Campanula. Some of the species, particularly *C. clematidea* have a rather unpleasing scent.

Codonopsis clematidea This is the species that is most frequently met with, although it is far from being the most attractive. In theory it can climb to 3 or 4 ft, but in practice it is usually between 1 and 2 ft high. The leaves are greyish-green and more or less egg-shaped. The flowers, which appear about July, are popularly described as ice-blue, but unpopularly as a dirty white. The plant will thrive in shady conditions, which enhances its value and all these climbing bellflowers have a curious fascination of their own.

Codonopsis convolvulacea This is a vigorous tuberous climber, capable of reaching to 7 ft high and, in the case of the more vigorous var. *forrestii*, even taller. The flowers, which are produced singly from the leaf axils are so expanded as to appear star-shaped rather than bell-shaped and are as much as 2 in. across. The stems branch slightly as they ascend. The flowers are lavender-blue in colour and appear from mid-summer over several weeks. Although the plant likes its roots to be shaded, I have seen it growing well on a south wall, planted underneath a Ceanothus, which was trained as a wall shrub. Good drainage is essential for this very attractive plant.

Codonopsis tangshen This is a fairly vigorous twiner, that can reach up to 10 ft in height and is not at all easy to acquire. It makes a cluster of long fleshy roots, and has greenish flowers, which are about 1½ in. long and which are richly spotted and marbled on the interior with purple. This species requires rather a large shrub over which to clamber and is not very suitable for the rock garden.

Codonopsis vinciflora This is rather like *C. convolvulacea*, but somewhat smaller both in growth and, though to a lesser extent, in the size of the flowers. This throws up a twining stem, which branches at the top and bears a solitary flower at the end of each branch. It requires to be grown in a sunny position and some people recommend sheltering the spot where the tuber is planted in the winter, as excessive damp may cause it to rot. However if plenty of gravel is included in the soil immediately under the tuber, this should prove effective. Nevertheless there seems little doubt that this is harder to keep in good condition than the other species. As its specific name implies the flowers are the colour of a Periwinkle (Vinca) and not dissimilar in shape, although they are pendent and more bell-shaped. I must add that, although it seems to do better in a sunny position, a friend of mine has it planted among a dense mass of dwarf rhododendrons, where it appears to thrive.

DOLICHOS

A genus of several twining shrubby and herbaceous plants, only one of which is sufficiently hardy to be considered here. That is the curiously named **Dolichos lablab,** the Hyacinth Bean. This is grown as though it were a Scarlet Runner Bean (Phaseolus) and, in the tropics, the pods are eaten in a similar manner. The plant is quite vigorous and has erect racemes of large pea-shaped purple or white flowers. The leaves are almost identical in appearance with those of the Scarlet Runner. This is an easy half-hardy climber and can be planted anywhere where it will receive a certain amount of sunshine. It is useful to clothe early-flowering shrubs.

HUMULUS

The Hop is a quick growing twining plant, which is useful for a screen, but is not otherwise particularly ornamental. There are two species in cultivation, **H. japonicus** and **H. lupulus.** The latter is the Hop of commerce, but there is a golden-leaved form, var. *aureus*, which is ornamental. *H. japonicus* has a form with spotted leaves (var. *variegatus*) which comes true from seed and is interesting to plant breeders as illustrating cytoplasmic inheritance; the variegation is transmitted only through the female plants. Hops are dioecious and both male and female plants are necessary to obtain seeds. If a male variegated plant fertilizes a green female, the offspring are green, but if a green male fertilizes a variegated female, the offspring are variegated. The Japanese Hop is frequently employed as an annual, although it is a perfectly good perennial, and so must be dug up, if it is only wanted temporarily. Although the female catkins, the Hops, are decorative, the plant is grown almost entirely for its vine-like leaves. It will grow in any soil, although it is naturally more luxuriant in deep humus-rich conditions.

PUERARIA

The Kudzu Vine, **Pueraria lobata,** is a very rapid growing plant, that is perennial in the mildest localities, but is used as an annual for clothing some eyesore temporarily. The genus is related to our Runner Beans, but it is only very rarely that the handsome 10 in. racemes of small violet-purple flowers are produced in this country, even in the greenhouse. If however the seeds are sown singly in pots in heat about the end of April and planted out as soon as there is no risk of frost, they may make as much as 20 ft of growth, before they are cut down by the frost. In mild districts, they will reappear in the spring, but otherwise they are to be regarded as annuals of exceptional vigour. There can be few plants that will make so much growth from seed in so short a time.

THUNBERGIA

A genus of tropical and sub-tropical climbers, some of great size and with very large flowers. The only species that can be grown out of doors is the short **Thunbergia alata,** one of many plants that are known as Black-eyed Susan. This is not a strong grower and will not exceed 4 ft in height. This is a half-hardy annual and needs to be started in gentle heat and planted in a warm situation, when the risk of frost has gone. The flowers have a tube about 1½ in. long and a five-lobed flat corolla. This is of various colours, ranging from white through pale yellow to nearly orange. The throat, the inside of the tube, is dark purple, which gives the black-eyed effect. The flowers are produced with some freedom from the leaf axils. Another species, perennial in the greenhouse, that is sometimes offered, is *T. gibsonii*, with bright orange flowers that are 1½ in. across, but I doubt whether this would flower very freely outside. *T. alata* itself may let you down, if the summer is cold. If we enjoy a reasonable season, this is a very pretty little twiner, flowering with great profusion from mid-July onwards. It needs to be put in a warm and sheltered position. It is again an excellent plant to climb up a wall-shrub, as its modest dimensions will cause no damage to its host.

This list of climbers of all sorts thus ends with a whimper, in the form of a half-hardy annual, rather than with a bang. Such is the result of following the alphabet. I can only hope that somewhere among all these plants you will find one to suit your garden. There are few surprises to be found in this list. Doubtless there are very many you have not heard of, but these plants tend to remain little-known for good reasons for the most part. The main exception seems to be *Schizandra rubrifolia* and I can conceive of no reason why this charming plant should not be as well-known as such stalwarts as Clematis and Wisteria. Many of the other climbers described may not have much floral beauty, but have attractive leaves and, in this connection, I would like to draw attention to some of the Chinese *Rubus* spp., particularly *R. henryi* and *R. setchuensis*. It is worth while to show a little enterprise and encourage the nurserymen to persist in growing unusual plants.

Index

Index

Figures in bold refer to plate numbers